AF480486

Abraham's Divided House

BY

DANIEL S. CARRERA

Copyright

eBook: 979-8950082368 ISBN

Paperback: 979-8950082375 ISBN

Hardcover: 979-8950082382 ISBN

TABLE OF CONTENTS

DEDICATION

This book is dedicated to several individuals who have played a major role in my development as a student, instructor, husband, and a Christian. What began as a doctoral dissertation has now grown into the book you are holding, and the people named here are the reason it exists at all. To my wife, Miranda Carrera, who played a significant role in my spiritual journey, leading me to Christ when we began dating in 2010. Through her witness and discipleship, I came to a deeper understanding of the gospel and committed my life to the Lord. In June 2014, I was rebaptized as a public affirmation of that transforming work of grace. Since that time, I have remained devoted to serving Christ faithfully in ministry, leadership, and theological study.

To Dr. Karol Hopson, who has been my instructor since my formal Christian journey began with Canaan Theological Seminary and Bible College (CTSC). Dr. Hopson's tireless dedication to teaching students both in the classroom and in Bible studies has been phenomenal. She kept me focused and was the impetus for my continued pursuit of a Bachelor of Science in Biblical Studies and the completion of my Doctor of Ministry through CTSC.

To Pastor Scharrod Wills, my pastor at True Vine Church of Jesus. Pastor Wills is an effective pastor who possesses a strong set of qualities that allow him to lead others to Christ. He displays great patience and is a tremendous administrator of the Word of God. He is a patient man who listens to others and strives to understand. The patience he displays is always evident during difficult situations or when listening to an opposing perspective, yet his foundation remains the indefensible Word of God.

To Overseer Sheldon Wills, the Overseer of True Vine Church of Jesus. Overseer Wills has a heart for the people and truly loves the Word of God, and it is evident by his devotion and the amount of time he has spent with me. Overseer Wills and I have prayed together every morning for the past five years, and I can unequivocally say he is the reason for my love for God. He is a mentor, an example, and a model that all Christians should emulate, and we toil every day in the Kingdom of God.

I would like to extend my heartfelt gratitude to Pastor Jerome Harper, whose generosity and trust opened doors for me at a time when I knew very little about ministry. He gave me the opportunity to stand before his congregation and grow, even when I was still learning, still uncertain, and still developing my voice.

His willingness to allow me to minister—not based on what I knew, but on what I was becoming—was a defining moment in my journey. That act of faith and leadership did more than give me an opportunity; it gave me confidence, direction, and a deeper sense of calling. I am truly thankful for his mentorship, his patience, and his belief in potential. His influence has left a lasting impact on both my life and ministry.

ABOUT THE AUTHOR

Dr. Daniel S. Carrera was born in Havana, Cuba, and grew up in the Catholic faith until a transforming encounter with Christ changed the course of his life. Through the witness and discipleship of his wife, Miranda, Daniel came to a deeper understanding of the gospel and committed his life to the Lord. In June 2014, he was rebaptized as a public declaration of that saving grace. Catholics carry a set of teachings passed down over the years that have been proclaimed as truth and safeguarded by the power of the Holy Spirit, teachings that guide conduct and order action. But when Daniel began attending True Vine Church of Jesus, a non-denominational church where the Bible is the central book of instruction, he found himself gaining a growing affinity for learning about the Triune God and understanding the Scriptures in a way he had never experienced before.

Upon graduation from the University of Wisconsin, Daniel entered the United States military in 1987, where he spent the next 22 years leading soldiers. Serving in the military was not just an ordinary job. It was a calling meant for people with a heart to serve, and there is no amount of compensation that can equal that kind of service. For Daniel, the transition from military servant leadership to servant leadership in God's Kingdom was a natural one, and it gave him a deep foundation for the work of bringing souls to Christ.

Daniel's educational journey reflects the same relentless pursuit that defines his faith. He holds two undergraduate degrees: a Bachelor of Science in Biological Studies from the University of Wisconsin (Parkside) and a Bachelor of Science in Biblical Studies from Canaan Theological Seminary and College. He earned two master's degrees: a Master of Organizational Leadership from Murray State University and a Master of Business Administration in Project Management from Strayer University. He completed his Doctor of Ministry through Canaan Theological Seminary and College. Daniel is married to the former Ms. Miranda Harding, and through a blended family they have two sons (Jonathan and Nicholas Carrera), two daughters (Melita and Marlene Harding), and one granddaughter (Janiyah Harding).

Chapter 1

OPENING THE ANCIENT FAMILY ALBUM

"And I will make of thee a great nation, and I will bless thee, and make thy name great; and thou shalt be a blessing." (Genesis 12:2, KJV)

There is a story that most of us have heard but few of us truly understand. It shows up on the evening news every week, buried inside the language of politics, territory, and military operations. It is a story that pastors are being asked about in Bible Study groups across the country. It is a story that seminary students are wrestling with in classrooms and that small group leaders are trying to navigate with their congregations.

It is the story of the Middle East conflict. What many people fail to recognize is that this is not, at its core, a political story. It is not fundamentally about borders, oil, or competing national interests. At its deepest level, it is a family story. And like every family story, it begins with a promise, a choice, and a consequence, one that has reverberated through thousands of years of human history and now confronts us in today's headlines.

A Promise and a Problem

The struggles of the Middle East today resulted from disobedience to God's law as discussed in Genesis 16. Abraham and his descendants were part of monotheistic cultures, but that disobedience resulted in the separation between Christianity, Judaism, and Islam. That is the thesis of this book, and it is one I have spent years studying, testing against Scripture, and confirming through both theological research and the witness of history.

The Middle East conflict started when Abraham's wife, Sarah, did not follow God's will. God had promised Abraham that he would become the father of a great nation (Genesis 12:2; 15:18). It was a breathtaking promise. Abraham and Sarah had no children at the time. Sarah was barren. The promise required something that Abraham and Sarah did not yet possess: patience and trust in God's timing.

Sarah, understandably anxious about her inability to bear children, suggested that Abraham have a child by her handmaid, Hagar (Genesis 16:1-2). Sarah thought she was 'helping

God out.' She had her own idea as to how Abraham could become the father of a great nation. She had a plan. But though she believed she was advancing the promise, she stepped outside of God's timing and assumed control of what only God had pledged to fulfill. As she developed that idea, she took control and offered Abraham her maid as a concubine, not merely as a cultural accommodation, but as a human attempt to accomplish a divine covenant. What appeared to be a practical solution became a turning point in redemptive history, revealing the perennial tension between promise and impatience, faith and flesh. From that moment, the covenant story carried not only the seed of promise, but the consequences of self-reliance, consequences that would reverberate through generations. Sarah may have done this because of unbelief (Genesis 18:11-15), but we cannot be sure of her motivation at that time.

Abraham and Hagar had a child, and they named him Ishmael. The initial thought for Sarah was that God had blessed her plan. But what followed revealed her sin. She became jealous, and Hagar fled. The Lord had more compassion than Sarah, and as Hagar was sent off into the wilderness, an angel of the Lord appeared to her. Then, fourteen years after Ishmael was born, God fulfilled His original promise. Sarah conceived, and Isaac was born (Genesis 16:16; 21:5). Isaac was the child of the covenant. But Ishmael was also Abraham's son, also loved, also blessed by God. And from these two sons, two great lineages emerged. Isaac's descendants became the Jewish people. Ishmael's descendants became the Arab peoples.

The ability to remain patient and wait for God to guide and order our steps will reduce civil unrest and promote unity and harmony. If Abraham had not been so impatient, all the Middle East headaches and hostility might have been spared. As we read through the book of Genesis, we should recognize that Abraham's impatience resulted in the separation of two nations: the Jewish nation and the Egyptian or Gentile nations. The critical point of this separation was the banishment of Abraham's first biological son, Ishmael, who was carried by Hagar.

Jacob, Esau, and the Sovereign Selection

The story does not end with Isaac and Ishmael. This book will highlight a number of passages revealing that Jacob (Israel), Abraham's grandson and the "selected seed," Isaac's son, would become the father of the nation of the Jewish people, Israel. Isaac's other son, Jacob's twin brother Esau, would become the father of the Edomites, the Palestinian people of today.

These two men, the twin sons of Isaac and Rebecca, were born "neither having done any good or evil." Yet the Lord, through what Scripture calls "sovereign selection," chose the younger twin, Jacob, to be served by the elder brother, Esau. The eldest son was meant to receive the "birthright" and the "blessing" from his father so that he would continue the heritage of his family. But God changed that. While the boys were still in their mother's womb, God determined that the elder would serve the younger. This act of what some have called "hatred" had nothing to do with salvation. It was about selection, about God choosing the elder son to serve the younger.

The Covenants That Shaped the Land

Moses outlines in Genesis chapters 12 through 17 the numerous promises God made with Abraham. The beginning of Chapter 12 highlights the story of Abraham and how God promised him a nation. In Chapter 15, God promises a son to Abraham. And in Chapter 17, the conditions of God's promise to Abraham are outlined, conditions that require obedience and faithfulness to the Word of God.

The Abrahamic Covenant established title to the land in the Middle East, and that title belongs to the Jewish people forever. Their use and enjoyment of the land, however, is conditional upon their obedience to God. This condition was established by a second covenant given through Moses right before Israel entered the land of Canaan. This Covenant (Mosaic Covenant) is recorded in Deuteronomy 28 through 30. In the Mosaic Covenant, God made it clear that the Jews' enjoyment of the land would depend upon their faithfulness to Him. If they were faithful, they would be richly blessed (Deuteronomy 28:1-14). But if they were unfaithful, they would be cursed in many ways (Deuteronomy 28:15-46).

Abraham Across Three Faiths

Abraham is a key founder of various religious traditions, and his bloodline is the genesis of the Middle East conflict. For the Jews, Abraham is the patriarch who received the covenant and bore the promised offspring that led to the twelve tribes of Israel. For Christians, Abraham is an example of salvation by faith and the conduit of blessing for all nations. For Islam, Abraham established the connection with Egyptian heritage that was a vital component of establishing the Arab nation. Ibrahim, the name by which Abraham is known in the Quran, is the second most referenced person in the Islamic holy book. One man. Three faiths. One family. And a conflict that has never stopped burning.

What You Will Find in These Pages

This book is organized into twelve chapters that walk you through the full arc of this story, from the birth of the world's primary religions to the headlines you are reading right now. We will begin by understanding the three great Abrahamic faiths and the land that God promised to Abraham's descendants. We will trace the genealogy of Abraham's family through Isaac and Ishmael, through Jacob and Esau, through the twelve tribes of Israel. We will explore how humanity became divided into Jews and Gentiles, and how the roots of the Israeli-Arab conflict stretch back thousands of years before the modern State of Israel was ever conceived.

This book will bring a narrative into the present moment, where the events of October 7, 2023, and their unfolding consequences have reminded the world that some conflicts run deeper than diplomacy and cannot be settled by human strategy alone. Throughout these pages, my goal is not to offer political commentary. My goal is to offer a biblical framework. A lens through which the believer can look at the chaos of the Middle East and see, with clarity, the hand of God at work in the story of Abraham's divided house. Let us walk carefully through what Scripture actually says.

Chapter 2

WHEN FAITH WAS YOUNG: THE BIRTH OF THREE RELIGIONS

"And without controversy great is the mystery of godliness: God was manifest in the flesh, justified in the Spirit, seen of angels, preached unto the Gentiles, believed on in the world, received up into glory." (1 Timothy 3:16, KJV)

Before we can understand the conflict in the Middle East, we must first understand what unites and divides the three great faiths that claim Abraham as their forefather. Islam, Christianity, and Judaism are not strangers to one another. They share a common ancestor, a common geography, and, to varying degrees, a common understanding of the one true God. And yet they have been at odds for centuries, sometimes violently so.

Religion is a set of organized beliefs, practices, and systems that most often relate to belief and worship of a force such as a personal God or gods or another supernatural being. While this is a basic definition, there are many different understandings of what religion is, and not all religions are centered on a belief in God, gods, or supernatural forces. Religion often involves cultural beliefs, worldviews, texts, prophecies, revelations, and morals that carry spiritual meaning to members of the faith, and it can encompass a range of practices including sermons, rituals, prayer, meditation, holy places, symbols, trances, and feasts.

Religion can serve a wide range of purposes. It can be a source of comfort and guidance. It can provide a basis for moral beliefs and behaviors. It can offer a sense of community and connection to tradition. Some research even suggests that it may influence health. It is equally important to understand that religion is an intrinsic part of human life. There are many different types of religions, including the major world traditions that are widely known as well as much lesser-known belief systems of smaller populations. Some represent monotheism, or the belief in a single god, while others are examples of polytheism, or the belief in multiple gods. The religions at the center of this book are Islam, Christianity, and Judaism.

Islam: Submission to the One God

Islam is the most widespread religion in the Middle East and one of the largest religions in the world. Research indicates that close to 94 percent of the Middle East's population identifies as Muslim (Boyett, 2016). The Middle East's Muslim population accounts for roughly 20 percent of the world's total Muslim population. The spread of Islam is closely linked with the history of the region, as converts established caliphates (an institution or public office governing under Islamic authority) with their own laws based on Islamic law. In the modern era, most of the nations in the Middle East use Islamic law as the basis of their legal system. The two main sects of Islam, Shia Islam and Sunni Islam, are both widely practiced in the region, with Sunni Islam having the larger following of the two.

Islam is based on the teachings of the Quran. Although it considers Muhammad to be the Seal of the prophets, Islam teaches that every prophet preached Islam, as the word Islam literally means "submission to God," the main concept preached by all Abrahamic prophets. The teachings of the Quran are believed by Muslims to be the direct and final revelation and words of Allah (the God, in classical Arabic). Islam, like Christianity, is a universal religion, meaning membership is open to anyone. Like Judaism, it has a strictly unitary conception of God, called tawhid, or "strict" monotheism.

Islam is the religion of allegiance to God that began with the prophet Muhammad, "peace be upon him." Once the name Muhammad is mentioned, there is an associated blessing that comes with his name. According to Islamic teaching, this religion was a way of life, called "din," and God's initial intention from the beginning. Human rebellion and sin meant that God continued to send prophets, including Moses (called Musa in Islam) and Jesus (called Isa by Muslims), to summon people back to the proper din.

The purpose of the life of Muslims is to please Allah alone as the One God. The religion of Islam is a complete code of life that firmly supports the concept of human well-being and urges every Muslim to behave in a consequential manner. The noblest message of morality is to respect the civil liberties of every individual in society while defining the duties of each person to perform in every aspect of life in order to create and nurture a peaceful and serene environment.

Most Muslims know and practice the five pillars of Islam: the Profession of Faith (Shahada), Daily Prayers (Salat), Alms-Giving (Zakat), Fasting during Ramadan (Saum), and Pilgrimage to Mecca (Hajj). However, like any building or structure, these five pillars must have a foundation. These pillars are the soul of Islam that make up their faith (Iman) and strength with their Allah. The five pillars are the body parts that one must know in order to practice Islamic faith with love and thankfulness.

Christianity: The Word Made Flesh

Another dominant religion that originated in the Middle East is Christianity, which traces its roots to modern-day Israel. Even though Christianity has its origins in the region, it is considered one of the minor religions in the area in the modern era, with its adherents accounting for only five percent of the region's population (Boyett, 2006). During the early twentieth century, Christians accounted for roughly 20 percent of the region's population. The only Middle Eastern nation with a Christian majority is Cyprus, where more than 70 percent of the population identifies as Christian (Boyett, 2006). The most popular Christian denomination in Cyprus is Eastern Orthodox Christianity, with the Greek residents of the country being the principal adherents.

Christianity began with the life, ministry, death, resurrection, and ascension of Jesus. The Apostle Paul describes how this came about in 1 Timothy 3:16, which reads: "And without controversy great is the mystery of godliness: God was manifest in the flesh, justified in the Spirit, seen of angels, preached unto the Gentiles, believed on in the world, received up into glory."

Christianity began in the first century as a sect within Judaism, initially led by Jesus. His followers viewed Him as the Messiah, as expressed in the Confession of Peter. After His crucifixion and death, they came to view Him as God incarnate, who was resurrected and will return at the end of time to judge the living and the dead and create an eternal Kingdom of God. Within a few decades, the new movement split from Judaism. Christian teaching is based on the Old and New Testaments of the Bible.

After several periods of alternating persecution and relative peace under different Roman administrations, Christianity became the state church of the Roman Empire in 380 AD, though it has been divided into various churches from its very beginning. An attempt was made by the Byzantine Empire to unify Christendom (the collective Christian culture), but this formally failed with the East-West Schism of 1054. In the sixteenth century, the birth and growth of Protestantism during the Reformation further split Christianity into many denominations. Christendom historically refers to the "Christian world": Christian states, Christian-majority countries, and the countries in which Christianity dominates, prevails, or is culturally intertwined with its inhabitants.

The Spread of Christendom

Since the spread of Christianity from the Levant countries (Lebanon, Syria, Iraq, Palestine, and Jordan) to Europe and North Africa during the early Roman Empire, Christendom has been divided along the lines of the pre-existing Greek East and Latin West. From the beginning of civilization, the Levant, the coastal region of the eastern Mediterranean stretching from Syria in the north to Egypt in the south, served as the crossroads of various peoples and cultures. From this important trade region, fundamental social and economic changes began spreading across the Middle East and the Mediterranean, leaving behind a rich heritage of unique material remains.

Consequently, different versions of the Christian religion arose with their own beliefs and practices, centered around the cities of Rome (Western Christianity, whose community was called Western or Latin Christendom) and Constantinople (Eastern Christianity, whose community was called Eastern Christendom). From the eleventh to the thirteenth centuries, Latin Christendom rose to the central role of the Western world. The history of the Christian world spans roughly 1,700 years and includes a variety of socio-political developments, as well as advances in the arts, architecture, literature, science, philosophy, and technology. The term Christendom usually refers to the Middle Ages and the Early Modern period, during which the Christian world represented a geopolitical power that stood alongside both the pagan and, especially, the Muslim world.

The Byzantine Empire, also referred to as the Eastern Roman Empire or Byzantium, was the continuation of the Roman Empire in its eastern provinces during Late Antiquity and the Middle Ages. Its capital city was Constantinople. It survived the fragmentation and fall of the Western Roman Empire in the fifth century AD and continued to exist for an additional thousand years until the fall of Constantinople to the Ottoman Empire in 1453. During most of its existence, the Byzantine Empire was the most powerful economic, cultural, and military force in Europe.

Judaism: The Ancient Covenant

One of Judaism's primary texts is the Tanakh, an account of the Israelites' relationship with God from their earliest history until the building of the Second Temple. The Tanakh is the Jewish Scriptures comprising the books of law (Torah), the prophets, and collected writings. The TaNaKh is the Hebrew Bible — the sacred Scriptures of Israel — and the foundation upon which the New Testament stands. The name itself is an acronym formed from three sections: Torah (Law), Nevi'im (Prophets), and Ketuvim (Writings). Together, they tell a unified story of creation, covenant, failure, judgment, hope, and promise.

The Torah begins with God as Creator and Covenant-Maker. In Genesis, humanity is formed in His image, called to reflect His glory, and invited into relationship. Through Abraham, God establishes a covenant promise: a people, a land, and a blessing that would ultimately extend to all nations. The Prophets interpret Israel's history. They confront idolatry, injustice, and covenant unfaithfulness, yet they also proclaim restoration. They speak of a coming King, a Servant, a new covenant, and a future in which God will dwell among His people. The Writings give voice to worship, wisdom, suffering, and hope. Through Psalms, Proverbs, and narratives of exile and return, they reveal the inner life of faith — how God's people wrestle with doubt, pain, and longing while clinging to promise.

The TaNaKh is not merely a collection of ancient texts. It is the unfolding account of God's redemptive plan — a story that begins in Eden, moves through covenant history, and anticipates a Messiah who will restore what was broken. For Christians, the TaNaKh is the soil from which the New Testament grows. It is the promise before the fulfillment, the shadow before the substance, the preparation before the appearing.

Abraham is hailed as the first Hebrew and the father of the Jewish people. One of his great-grandsons was Judah, from whom the religion ultimately takes its name. The Israelites were initially a number of tribes who lived in the Kingdom of Israel and the Kingdom of Judah. After being conquered and exiled, some members of the Kingdom of Judah eventually returned to Israel. They later formed an independent state under the Hasmonean dynasty before becoming a client kingdom of the Roman Empire, which eventually conquered the state and dispersed its inhabitants.

The Hasmonean dynasty takes its name from the family of the rebel leader and priest, Mattathias, who began to throw off Seleucid rule. Upon his death, his sons continued the rebellion and were eventually successful in gaining Jewish autonomy under the Seleucids and then, with the disintegration of the Seleucid Empire, full Jewish independence. Simon, the brother of Judah Maccabee and son of Mattathias, was the first Hasmonean ruler of an autonomous state. The Hasmoneans are also called Asmoneans. The name Hasmonean comes from the Hebrew word chashman, meaning "wealthy." According to the historian Josephus, a priest named Chashman, from the family of Jehoiarib (1 Chronicles 24:7), was the ancestor of the Hasmoneans. Their history is found in the works of Josephus and the apocryphal books of 1 and 2 Maccabees.

Zionism and the Modern Tension

The Middle East is home to some of the world's most chaotic and violent conflict zones, including Libya, Syria, Yemen, and Iraq, as well as simmering tensions in states such as Israel and Lebanon. And while these conflicts usually have multiple causes, religion and religious hostilities are certainly important factors. Zionism is Israel's national ideology. Zionists believe Judaism is a nationality as well as a religion, and that Jews deserve their own state in their ancestral homeland, Israel, in the same way the French people have France or the Chinese people have China. It is what brought Jews back to Israel in the first place, and it is also at the heart of what concerns Arabs and Palestinians about the Israeli state.

Though Zionists all agree that Israel should exist, they have long disagreed on what its government should look like. In the most general terms, the Zionist left, which dominated the country's politics until the late 1970s, is inclined to trade Israeli-controlled land for peace with Arab nations, favors more government intervention in the economy, and prefers a secular government over a religious one. The Zionist right, which currently holds commanding positions in the Israeli government and popular opinion, tends to be more skeptical of "land-for-peace" deals, more libertarian on the economy, and more comfortable mixing religion and politics.

Arabs and Palestinians generally oppose Zionism, as the explicitly Jewish character of the Israeli state means that Jews have privileges that others do not. For instance, any Jew anywhere in the world can become an Israeli citizen, a right not extended to any other class of person. Arabs often see Zionism as a form of colonialism and racism aimed at appropriating Palestinian land and systematically disenfranchising the Palestinians who remain. Arab states actually pushed through a UN General Assembly resolution labeling Zionism "a form of racism and racial discrimination" in 1975, though it was repealed 16 years later.

The Reality on the Ground

A Pew Research Center study, relying on information from 2014 (the most recent year data were available at the time), carefully catalogued hostilities in the region's 20 countries. For the first time since these reports were published in 2007, the study took into account activity by the Islamic militant group known as ISIS, which declared in June 2014 that it had established a caliphate in parts of Iraq and Syria. The findings were sobering. The region continued to have the highest levels of religious hostilities in the world. In 2014, the median level of religious hostilities in the Middle East and North Africa reached a level four times that of the global median. The types of hostilities included religion-related armed conflict, sectarian violence, and other forms of religion-related intimidation or abuse.

Six countries in the region had "very high" levels of religious hostilities during that year, including Israel, Iraq, Syria, Yemen, Lebanon, and the Palestinian territories. Violent acts in Iraq by both Sunni- and Shia-dominated groups and militias, including ISIS, led to killings, kidnappings, harassment, intimidation, and displacement. The region had the largest share of countries experiencing religion-related terrorism in 2014. Terrorist activities became more lethal in Israel in particular, where attacks resulted in over 50 casualties. Members of the Abu Ali

Mustafa Brigades claimed responsibility for one of these attacks, which killed at least five people, including four rabbis, in November of that year.

There were reports of ethnic cleansing related to religion in Iraq. Islamic State militants engaged in what Amnesty International called a "systematic campaign of ethnic cleansing" that targeted religious and ethnic minorities. The State Department reported instances of the group seeking to "exterminate" Shia Muslims and religious minorities by targeting Shia mosques and communities. The group massacred at least 500 Yazidi civilians in August 2014, disposing of their bodies in mass graves. Harassment of Christians and Jews by both government forces and social groups increased in 2014. Christians were harassed in 16 out of 20 countries in the region (up from 15 countries in 2013), and Jews were harassed in 18 countries (up from 17 the previous year). In Jordan, some converts from Islam to Christianity reported having to worship in secret for fear of social stigma. Muslims also faced harassment in 17 out of 20 countries surveyed, unchanged from the previous year.

Perhaps most strikingly, about 800,000 more people were displaced by religion-related armed conflict in 2014 than in the previous year. More than 19 million people in the Middle East and North Africa were displaced due to such conflicts, up from 18.2 million in 2013. These numbers tell a story that statistics alone cannot fully convey. Behind every displacement figure is a family. Behind every harassment report is a human being whose freedom to worship has been violated. And behind all of it is the ancient family story we are tracing in these pages. Understanding the roots of these three faiths, and the way they have intersected and collided across the centuries, is the first step toward understanding why the Middle East remains the most contested piece of geography on earth.

Chapter 3

THE LAND GOD PROMISED

"In the same day the LORD made a covenant with Abram, saying, Unto thy seed have I given this land, from the river of Egypt unto the great river, the river Euphrates." (Genesis 15:18, KJV)

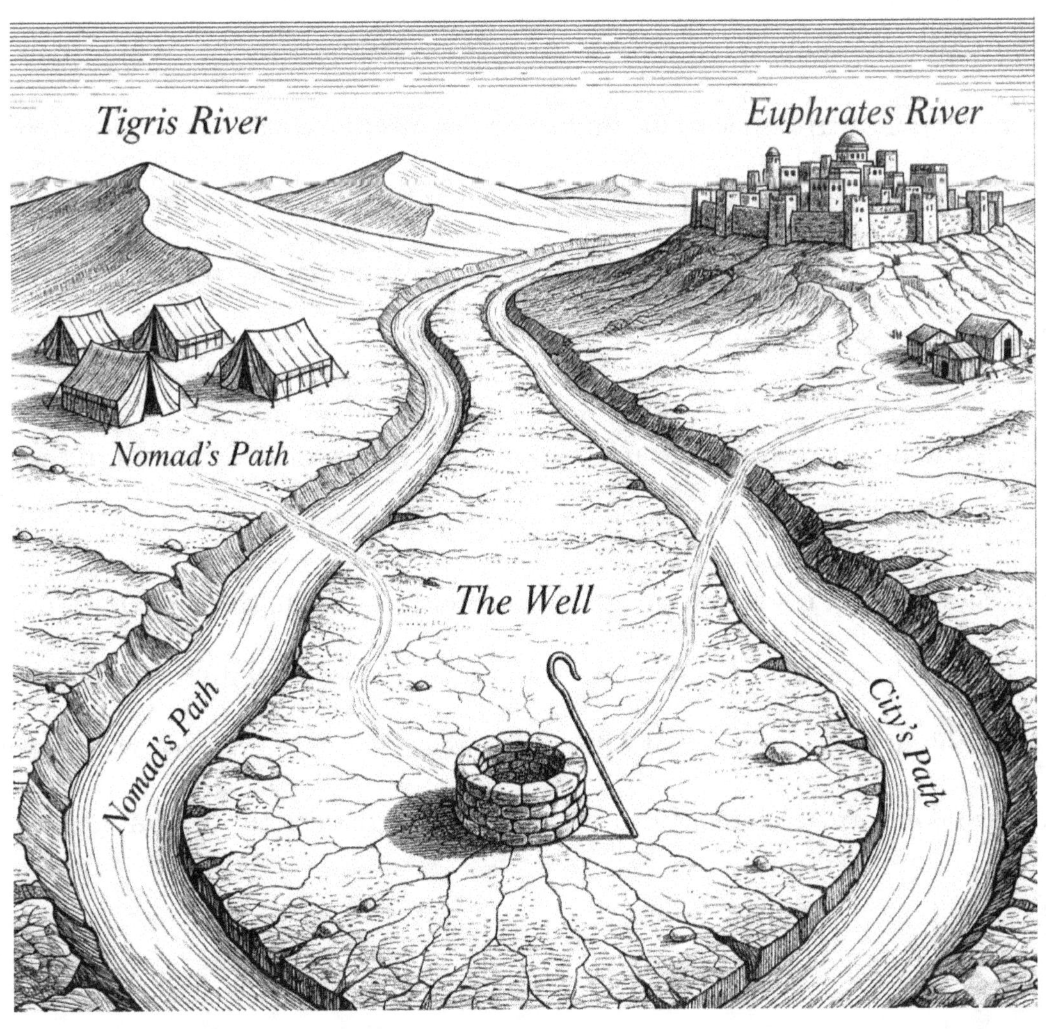

The Middle East encompasses the lands around the southern and eastern shores of the Mediterranean Sea. Although primarily located in western Asia, it is a transcontinental region because portions of its territory are also found in northern Africa and a tiny part of southeastern Europe. This area also includes what is sometimes referred to as the Levant. The term refers to "the area of the rising of the sun," from the perspective of the western Mediterranean. The Levant is the eastern Mediterranean area now covered by Israel, Lebanon, part of Syria, and western Jordan. In antiquity, the southern part of the Levant, or Palestine, was called Canaan.

By the mid-twentieth century, a common definition of the Middle East encompassed the states or territories of Turkey, Cyprus, Syria, Lebanon, Iraq, Iran, Israel, the West Bank, the Gaza Strip, Jordan, Egypt, Sudan, Libya, and the various states and territories of Arabia proper: Saudi Arabia, Kuwait, Yemen, Oman, Bahrain, Qatar, and the Trucial States (now the United Arab Emirates). Subsequent events have tended to enlarge the number of lands included in the definition. The three North African countries of Tunisia, Algeria, and Morocco are closely connected in sentiment and foreign policy with the Arab states. In addition, geographic factors often require statesmen and others to take account of Afghanistan and Pakistan in connection with the affairs of the Middle East.

Arabs are the majority ethnic group in this part of the world. Thirteen of the countries in the region are part of the Arab League, a loose confederation of twenty-two Arab nations whose broad mission is to improve coordination among its members on matters of common interest. The league was chartered in response to concerns about postwar colonial divisions of territory as well as strong opposition to the emergence of a Jewish state on Palestinian territory. It is important to note that Arabs and Jews are related. Both trace their lineage back to Abraham.

The Cradle of Civilization

The Middle East is widely recognized as the cradle of civilization. The Garden of Eden, where God placed the first man and woman, may have been in southern Mesopotamia (modern Iraq) near the Tigris and Euphrates Rivers (Genesis 2:14). The cradle of civilization is any location where civilization is understood to have independently emerged. According to current thinking, there was no single "cradle" of civilization; rather, several cradles developed independently. Mesopotamia, Ancient Egypt, Ancient India, and Ancient China are believed to be the earliest in the Old World. The Old World consists of Africa, Europe, and Asia, or Afro-Eurasia, regarded collectively as the part of the world known to its inhabitants before contact with the Americas, which are therefore called the New World.

Following the great universal flood that came upon the world, the ark that protected Noah and his family came to rest *"on the mountains of Ararat"* (Genesis 8:4). These mountains are found in modern Turkey. A large portion of the Middle East is sometimes referred to as the Promised Land because much of it was promised by God to Abraham and his descendants (Genesis 15:18-21). This was where the ancient nation of Israel, including its capital city of Jerusalem, was located.

The Middle East is where the Old Testament was inspired by God to be written and the home of its prophets. It is also where Jesus conducted His ministry and where Muhammad, the founder of Islam, lived and died. With so much sacred history concentrated in one region, it is easy to understand why Judaism, Christianity, and Islam all have their origins here.

A Long-Simmering Family Feud

Many people today do not understand that the tensions between the Jews and the Arab countries in the Middle East are a long-simmering family feud. The rift began long ago, when Abram (later called Abraham, Genesis 17:5) began raising his family. Initially unable to have children with his wife Sarai (later called Sarah, Genesis 17:15), Abraham decided to follow a custom that had developed at that time in order to produce an heir. At the urging of his wife, Abraham fathered a child through Hagar, his wife's Egyptian handmaid (Genesis 16:1-2). Shortly after Hagar conceived, tensions between Sarah and Hagar boiled over. Scripture tells us:

"And when she [Hagar] saw that she had conceived, her mistress [Sarah] became despised in her eyes." (Genesis 16:4)

After Sarah confronted Abraham about the issue, he gave his wife permission to deal with Hagar as she pleased:

"And when Sarai dealt harshly with her, she fled from her presence." (Genesis 16:6)

Then God told Hagar to return to her mistress and that she would bear a son who should be called Ishmael. After his birth, Hagar and Ishmael remained with Abraham and Sarah. God then appeared to Abraham and told him that he would bear a son through his wife Sarah. Fourteen years after Ishmael's birth, Isaac was born (Genesis 16:16; 21:5). On the day Isaac was weaned, "Abraham made a great feast" (Genesis 21:8). The joyous occasion was soon marred with tension between Sarah and her handmaid.

"Sarah saw the son of Hagar the Egyptian, whom she had borne to Abraham, scoffing. Therefore she said to Abraham, 'Cast out this bondwoman and her son;

for the son of this bondwoman shall not be heir with my son, namely with Isaac.'"

(Genesis 21:9-10)

Abraham was in a difficult position. He did not want to send Ishmael away. But with the admonition from God to listen to Sarah, and with assurance from God that Ishmael's descendants would also become a nation, Abraham did so (Genesis 21:11-14). Even though Isaac received Abraham's wealth (Genesis 25:5), God also blessed Ishmael. The child of Hagar and Abraham had twelve sons, who each fathered nations (Genesis 25:12-16), just as God had previously said (Genesis 17:20). Ishmael's descendants are the Arab peoples today. From this rocky start in a household with two mothers, jealousies and rivalries have continued through the ages between Ishmael's descendants (the Arabs) and the descendants of Isaac's grandson Judah (the Jews).

Chapter 4

ABRAHAM: THE FATHER WHO CHANGED EVERYTHING

"Get thee out of thy country, and from thy kindred, and from thy father's house, unto a land that I will shew thee." (Genesis 12:1, KJV)

COMPLETE GENEALOGY OF ABRAHAM

From Terah to the Twelve Tribes of Israel & the Chiefs of Edom

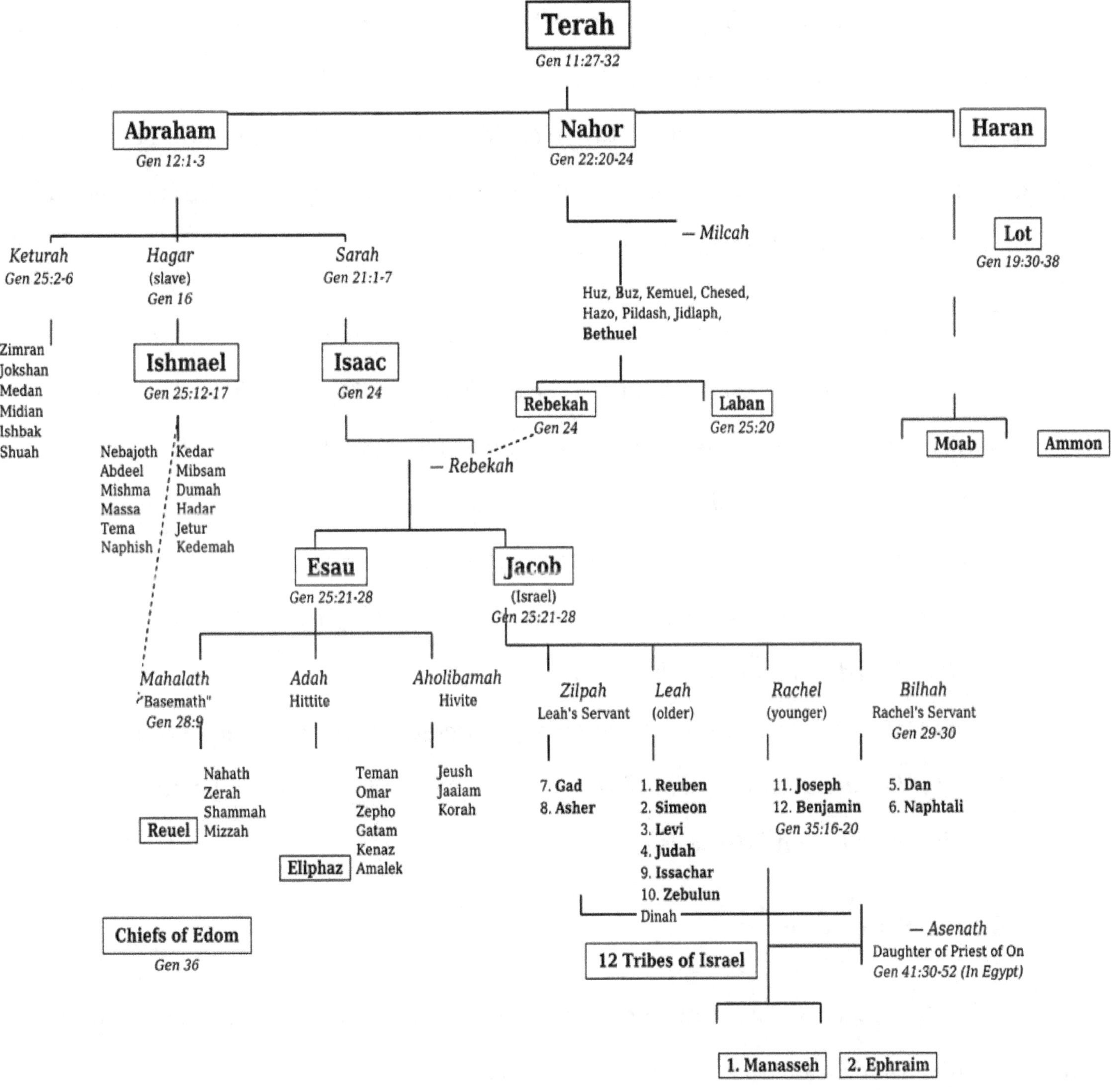

The Genealogy of Abraham

Abraham was born after the Great Flood of Noah. Terah, Abraham's father, was the ninth-generation descendant of Shem, one of Noah's three sons who rode with him on the ark. Abraham had two brothers, named Nahor and Haran. The Bible records that Terah, probably upon Abraham's suggestion, decided to relocate with his family from Ur of the Chaldees to the land of Canaan. Unfortunately, Terah died before ever reaching Canaan. He died in Haran, a city located along what is today the border area between the modern states of Syria and Turkey. Scripture records the full genealogical account in Genesis 11:27-32:

"Now these are the generations of Terah: Terah begat Abram, Nahor, and Haran; and Haran begat Lot. And Haran died before his father Terah in the land of his nativity, in Ur of the Chaldees. And Abram and Nahor took them wives: the name of Abram's wife was Sarai; and the name of Nahor's wife, Milcah, the daughter of Haran, the father of Milcah, and the father of Iscah. But Sarai was barren; she had no child. And Terah took Abram his son, and Lot the son of Haran his son's son, and Sarai his daughter in law, his son Abram's wife; and they went forth with them from Ur of the Chaldees, to go into the land of Canaan; and they came unto Haran, and dwelt there. And the days of Terah were two hundred and five years: and Terah died in Haran." (Genesis 11:27-32, KJV)

The Call and the Covenant

When God began working with Abram (his name was later changed to Abraham), God gave him a command and an amazing promise. The command was:

"Get out of your country, from your family and from your father's house, to a land that I will show you" (Genesis 12:1).

Explaining the promise, He would give Abraham in exchange for his obedience, God continued:

"I will make you a great nation; I will bless you and make your name great; and you shall be a blessing. I will bless those who bless you, and I will curse him who curses you; and in you all the families of the earth shall be blessed." (Genesis 12:2-3)

This promise had multiple components, including the promise of numerous descendants, fame, divine protection, and the assurance that Abraham, through his descendants, would be a blessing to all people. Abraham's son Isaac and grandson Jacob were described as *"heirs with him of the same promise."* There were multiple components that were part of this promise. Indeed, it is also acceptable to refer to these components as promises to Abraham. This is how many translations of the Bible, including the New King James Version, translate Paul's statement to the Galatians: *"Now to Abraham and his Seed were the promises made"* (Galatians 3:16).

The promises to Abraham were both physical and spiritual in nature. Physically, Abraham's descendants would become a great nation. The spiritual blessing to all people was fulfilled in the coming of Jesus, the Messiah, a descendant of Abraham, through whom people of all nationalities may receive salvation (Acts 4:10-12; Galatians 3:16).

A Land Forever

When Abraham left his country for the land God had promised to show him, *"he went out, not knowing where he was going"* (Hebrews 11:8). After Abraham arrived in the land God wanted him to see, God announced that He would give this land to his descendants. As Abraham obeyed and grew in faith, God continued to reveal to him the blessings he and his descendants would receive:

"The LORD said to Abram, after Lot had separated from him: 'Lift your eyes now and look from the place where you are, northward, southward, eastward, and westward; for all the land which you see I give to you and your descendants forever. And I will make your descendants as the dust of the earth; so that if a man could number the dust of the earth, then your descendants also could be numbered. Arise, walk in the land through its length and its width, for I give it to you.'" (Genesis 13:14-17)

Once Abram heard this command from the Lord, he moved his tent and established a dwelling and built an altar unto the Lord. God had promised to bless Abraham, and this soon became apparent through Abraham's personal wealth. Adding to what He had previously spoken, God now told this patriarch that his descendants would be numerous and that He was giving this land to Abraham and his descendants forever. God then encouraged Abraham to walk through the land, to survey the gift he was being given.

The Promise of Countless Descendants

Later, God expanded the promise even further. In response to Abraham's statement that he was childless and that a servant stood as his heir, God reassured him:

"And behold, the word of the LORD came to him, saying, 'This one shall not be your heir, but one who will come from your own body shall be your heir.' Then He brought him outside and said, 'Look now toward heaven, and count the stars if you are able to number them.' And He said to him, 'So shall your descendants be.' And he believed in the LORD, and He accounted it to him for righteousness. ... On the same day the LORD made a covenant with Abram, saying: 'To your descendants I

have given this land, from the river of Egypt to the great river, the River Euphrates."' (Genesis 15:4-6, 18)

A significant detail here is that Abraham believed that what God had promised would indeed come about. Scripture tells us that this faith was credited to him as righteousness. God repeated His promise of land for Abraham's descendants, this time formalizing it with a covenant that included specific geographical boundaries, from the river of Egypt to the great river Euphrates.

The Expanding Promises

The following are additional promises that were specifically given to Abraham by the Lord, each one building upon the last and deepening the covenant relationship between God and His chosen patriarch: God's promises to Abraham and Sarah as father and mother of many nations (Genesis 17:1-8, 15-16). God's decision to share His plans with Abraham directly (Genesis 18:17-18). The birth of Isaac as the fulfillment of the promise (Genesis 21:1-3). The promise of *"the gate of their enemies"* (Genesis 22:16-18). And God's extension of His promise to Abraham's descendants through Isaac and Jacob (Genesis 26:3-5; 27:26-29; 28:13-14; 35:11-12).

Do These Promises Still Matter?

It is important to understand that today it is commonly accepted among believers that Jesus Christ was the fulfillment of God's promise to bless all families of the earth through Abraham. It is also acknowledged that Abraham's descendants multiplied and eventually became the ancient nations of Israel and Judah. But the question remains: does God's promise to Abraham have any significance today?

While many people readily acknowledge that the blessing of Jesus Christ to all peoples continues today, they do not know whether the physical promises to Abraham's descendants are still applicable. Some believe that the blessings were fulfilled in ancient times and that there is no continuance of the physical promises. But what the Bible teaches is that the physical blessings to these people will continue until and after Christ's return. Genesis 49:1 presupposes that the twelve sons of Jacob would grow into prominent nations and that they would exist *"in the last days."*

The promises God made to Abraham were not temporary. They were not conditional on a timeline. They were, and remain, forever. And it is within the tension between those promises, between the descendants who claim them and the nations that contest them, that the story of the Middle East continues to unfold. In the next chapter, we will turn our attention to the son who was born outside of God's promise but within God's compassion: Ishmael, the son of the bondwoman, and the father of the Arab peoples.

Chapter 5

THE SON OF THE BONDWOMAN: ISHMAEL'S STORY

"Cast out this slave woman with her son, for the son of this slave woman shall not be heir

with my son Isaac." (Genesis 21:10)

A Father's Love, A Father's Obedience

On the day Isaac was weaned, Abraham prepared a great feast. When Sarah saw Hagar's son, the Egyptian woman who had borne a child to Abraham, laughing, she said to Abraham, *"Cast out this slave woman and her son, for the son of this slave woman shall not share the inheritance with my son Isaac"* (Genesis 21:10). Abraham was not happy with Sarah's response (Genesis 21:11). He cared about Sarah, but he did not share her view that Hagar and Ishmael should be sent away. Ishmael was his firstborn son. But God spoke to Abraham on this issue: *"Be not displeased because of the boy and because of your slave woman. Whatever Sarah says to you, do as she tells you, for through Isaac shall your offspring be named. And I will make a nation of the son of the slave woman also, because he is your offspring"* (Genesis 21:12–13). God's promise to make another nation from Ishmael began to be fulfilled when Ishmael had twelve sons who presided over twelve tribes (Genesis 25:16).

Abraham obeyed the Lord. Scripture records, *"So Abraham rose early in the morning and took bread and a skin of water and gave it to Hagar, placing it on her shoulder along with the child, and sent her away"* (Genesis 21:14). As far as the biblical narrative reveals, Abraham did not see Ishmael again, though Ishmael was present at Abraham's burial (Genesis 25:9). While Abraham clearly expressed compassion for his son, he ultimately demonstrated obedience when God required something different from his personal desire. In this, Abraham modeled a humility of surrender, submitting his emotions to divine instruction, a lesson that continues to speak to believers today.

God calls us to obedience, and that requires a willingness to give up personal desires in order to follow Him. Those who love the Lord know that the Lord's will is what matters most. Abraham obeyed God and was known as *"Friend of God"* (James 2:23), and his faith followed God's will, even in the most difficult of times.

What the Bible Tells Us About Ishmael

Ishmael is considered a patriarch of Islam based upon legends that have developed around him and information found in the Qur'an. But what does the Bible tell us about Ishmael? In Genesis 17, Abraham is 99 years old, making Ishmael approximately 13. God appeared to Abraham once again and reiterated the promise that he would be the father of many nations. God told Abraham that Sarah, then 90 years old, would have a son. Abraham had a hard time believing this and asked that God would fulfill His promises through Ishmael (verse 18). From this we can see that Abraham genuinely loved Ishmael. However, God said the promise would be fulfilled through a son that Sarah would bear:

"Your wife Sarah will bear you a son, and you will call him Isaac. I will establish my covenant with him as an everlasting covenant for his descendants after him.

And as for Ishmael, I have heard you: I will surely bless him; I will make him fruitful and will greatly increase his numbers. He will be the father of twelve rulers, and I will make him into a great nation. But my covenant I will establish with Isaac, whom Sarah will bear to you by this time next year." (Genesis 17:19–21)

In Genesis 21, Sarah's son Isaac was born, and once again problems arose. Sarah saw Ishmael mocking the young Isaac, and she demanded action from Abraham: *"Get rid of that slave woman and her son, for that woman's son will never share in the inheritance with my son Isaac"* (verse 10).

"The matter distressed Abraham greatly because it concerned his son. But God said to him, 'Do not be so distressed about the boy and your slave woman. Listen to whatever Sarah tells you, because it is through Isaac that your offspring will be reckoned. I will make the son of the slave into a nation also, because he is your offspring.'" (Genesis 21:11–13)

Once again, Abraham's love for Ishmael comes through, and once again God promises to bless the boy. Abraham gathered some provisions and sent Hagar and Ishmael away. After the provisions had been exhausted, Hagar and Ishmael were overcome with grief, certain they would die in the desert.

"God heard the boy crying, and the angel of God called to Hagar from heaven and said to her, 'What is the matter, Hagar? Do not be afraid; God has heard the boy crying as he lies there. Lift the boy up and take him by the hand, for I will make him into a great nation.' Then God opened her eyes and she saw a well of water.

So she went and filled the skin with water and gave the boy a drink." (Genesis 21:17–19)

Once again, God appeared to Hagar and promised that Ishmael would become a great nation. And then Scripture tells us something quietly remarkable: *"God was with the boy as he grew up. He lived in the desert and became an archer. While he was living in the Desert of Paran, his mother got a wife for him from Egypt"* (verses 20–21). Upon Abraham's death, he left everything to Isaac, but Ishmael did help his half-brother bury Abraham (Genesis 25:9). Genesis 25:12–18 lists the descendants of Ishmael. They were indeed numerous, divided into twelve tribes, and, as God had earlier revealed, *"they lived in hostility toward all the tribes related to them"* (verse 18). Ishmael lived a total of 137 years (verse 17).

Ishmael After Genesis

Genesis 25 is the last mention of Ishmael as an individual; however, his descendants continue to be mentioned in relation to Israel. Esau married a descendant of Ishmael because his mother did not want him to marry Canaanite women (see Genesis 28:6–8; 36:3). Ishmaelites are mentioned as a people group in Genesis 37, where Joseph's brothers sold him to Ishmaelite traders who took him to Egypt as a slave. Ishmaelites are mentioned incidentally a few more times in the Old Testament, as well as other unrelated men named Ishmael, but the New Testament is silent about him.

Islamic tradition states that Abraham took Hagar and Ishmael to Mecca, and Ishmael is considered a patriarch of Islam. While it is not accurate to say that all Arabs are descended from Ishmael, there is still a great deal of strife between the descendants of Isaac and those who see Ishmael as their father. One wonders how things might have been different had Abraham simply trusted God to bring about His promise without any added "help" from Abraham and Sarah.

The Descendants of Ishmael

Ishmael was the first son of Abraham, born of Sarah's maidservant Hagar in an attempt to bring into the world the son God had promised to Abraham and Sarah. Later, Isaac was born to Abraham and Sarah, and Hagar and Ishmael were driven away because of Ishmael's attitude toward Isaac (Genesis 21:9–10, 14). But God still had plans for Ishmael, the son of an Egyptian woman considered to be a Gentile.

God promised Hagar that Ishmael, as a son of Abraham, would become a great nation (Genesis 21:17–18). The fulfillment is recorded in Genesis 25:12–18: Ishmael had twelve sons who became great rulers and eventually a nation of people. That came about in this way: Hagar, who was Egyptian herself, found a wife from Egypt for her son, and Ishmael settled in the Desert of Paran (Genesis 21:21). Ishmael's descendants *"settled in the area from Havilah to Shur, near the border of Egypt as you go toward Ashur"* (Genesis 25:18). The Bible lists Ishmael's twelve sons as Nebaioth, Kedar, Adbeel, Mibsam, Mishma, Dumah, Massa, Hadad, Tema, Jetur, Naphish, and Kedemah (verses 13–15).

The area of Havilah where Ishmael's descendants lived is in the northern part of the Arabian Peninsula. Shur is a wilderness area between Beersheba in the Negev Desert and Egypt. Isaiah 60:7 mentions the descendants of Nebaioth and Kedar as those who raise flocks. The descendants of Ishmael became known as *"Arabs,"* which basically means *"nomads."* From the beginning, the descendants of Ishmael were a warlike people, as *"they lived in hostility toward all the tribes related to them"* (Genesis 25:18). This fulfilled God's earlier word that Ishmael would be *"a wild donkey of a man; his hand will be against everyone and everyone's hand against him, and he will live in hostility toward all his brothers"* (Genesis 16:12).

In terms of present-day geography, the region described in these passages would encompass much of what is now Saudi Arabia, particularly the northern and western portions of the Arabian Peninsula. The wilderness of Shur would fall near the modern border region between Egypt and Israel, including areas of the Sinai Peninsula. Havilah is commonly associated with territory extending across northern Arabia toward the Persian Gulf. The tribes descending from Nebaioth and Kedar are historically linked with regions that today include parts of Saudi Arabia, Jordan, and southern Iraq. Over time, these nomadic desert tribes became identified with the broader Arab peoples of the Middle East. Thus, the biblical record places Ishmael's descendants across territories that now form a significant portion of the modern Arab world.

Later, others settled in the Arabian Peninsula as well, including the descendants of Keturah's sons (1 Chronicles 1:32–33) and some of Esau's descendants, among them the Amalekites (Genesis 36:12). There is a popular theory common among Muslims and some Christians that Arabian Muslims are direct descendants of Ishmael. There is discussion that highlights Muhammad was a major proponent of this idea, claiming to be a descendant of Ishmael according to the Qur'an. Although some modern Arabians could trace their lineage back to Ishmael, not all Arabians are descendants of Ishmael as some claim.

We know from the Bible that God made Ishmael into a great nation. His descendants can share in the blessings of Abraham by putting their faith in Jesus Christ for salvation. That is the promise that remains open to every son and daughter of Abraham, whether through Isaac or through Ishmael.

Chapter 6

THE SON OF PROMISE: ISAAC AND THE BLESSING

"The voice is the voice of Jacob, but the hands are the hands of Esau!" (Genesis 27:22)

Isaac's Two Blessings

Isaac essentially had two blessings to confer. One was a temporal blessing—the promise of material prosperity and the physical benefits of life in this world. Though significant, this was not the ultimate good. The second was the greater and enduring blessing: the spiritual inheritance of the covenant, which Isaac had received from his father Abraham. This covenantal blessing carried the promise of divine favor, redemptive purpose, and the unfolding plan of God.

The blessing carried the right to become the head of the family after the death of the father. Unfortunately, Isaac was attempting to go against God's will. The prophecy given to Rebekah before the birth of Esau and Jacob had stated clearly that Jacob would be the ruling son. The truly spiritual blessings, Isaac had always intended to give Jacob and would still do so. However, Esau persisted, and Isaac relented and blessed Esau. The blessing of Esau was not a true blessing but a conditional blessing.

Esau's Evil Ways

Although Jacob had gone to the academy of Shem and Eber to study the teachings of God, Esau refused to do anything of the sort. He led his life in his own way and became more estranged from his father's teachings. Yet he honored his father and tried to appear an obedient and loving son, ready to comply with his father's every wish, if it did not involve him in studying and learning. Isaac could not and did not see Esau's godless behavior, for his eyes were dim with age, and he was confined to his tent.

When studying Genesis 11, we learn that Abram (Abraham) was born 352 years after the Flood. Noah died only two years before the birth of Abraham! Shem and Eber were still alive, even during Jacob's life! Truly, Shem is the father of all the sons of Eber, father of the Hebrews. We do not know for certain whether they ever met and spoke with Abraham, with Isaac, and with Jacob (or even with Ishmael and Esau), but it is likely, and they would have had eyewitness accounts of pre-Flood and post-Flood people and events, as God maintained His witness and passed it on to His chosen persons and family.

Noah was the tenth from Adam and was protected through the judgment of the Flood; Abraham was tenth from Shem, who also was saved from the Flood. Chapter 12 carries on with God's redemptive plan, choosing Abram – son of Eber, son of Shem, son of Noah — from among all the Gentiles, through whom He would bless the world through covenant and promise – and lots of controversy. Rebekah, however, saw everything. She observed the quiet and pleasing ways of Jacob and watched with alarm the true nature of her firstborn son Esau. For her there could be no doubt as to which of her children had chosen the right way.

Rebekah's Ploy

After the death of Shem, Jacob returned to his father's house, and Esau, too, came home from Seir. Isaac had grown old and weak and felt that the time had come for him to give his sons his last blessings. Still believing that he could entrust Esau with the task of carrying on Abraham's tradition, Isaac told Esau to hunt some deer meat, prepare a meal for him, and receive his blessings. Gladly, Esau took his bow and quiver and went out into the field.

Rebekah had heard what her husband told Esau, and in a moment her resolve was taken. Esau should not receive the blessing which, as she believed, belonged even from his birth to her younger and wiser son. She went to Jacob, and hastily related to him what she had heard, and then she suggested to him that he prepare some meat and bring it to his father in the disguise of his brother Esau. Jacob was reluctant to trick his father, even though he knew his mother was right. But Rebekah ordered him to do as she said, taking full responsibility for the act. Jacob did not dare to refuse his mother, and so he fetched two tender kids from the flock, and Rebekah prepared them so that they tasted like deer meat. Then she dressed her younger son in the festive garments of Esau, and to render the resemblance perfect, she covered his smooth neck and hands with the skins of the kids. She then put the meal into his hands and sent him to his father.

The Blessing

Isaac wondered at his son's early return, and at his soft-spoken and pious address. Feeling Jacob's arms and neck, Isaac exclaimed: *"The voice is the voice of Jacob, but the hands are the hands of Esau!"* Isaac ate the meat Jacob brought him. Then he blessed his son with the words:

"And may the Lord give you of the dew of the heavens and of the fatness of the earth

and an abundance of corn and wine. Nations shall serve you and kingdoms shall bow down to you; you shall be a master over your brothers, and your mother's sons shall bow down to you. Those who curse you shall be cursed, and those who bless you shall be blessed!" (Genesis 27:28–29)

Esau Returns

Hardly had Jacob left Isaac, when Esau returned from the hunt. He prepared the deer meat and brought it to his father. He soon learned what had happened in the meantime and cried with anger and disappointment. Isaac blessed him too, giving him the right to throw off the yoke of his brother whenever his brother strayed from the path of God. But Esau hated Jacob, and Jacob evaded the rage of his brother by returning to Eber to study under his care.

The Significance of the Patriarchal Blessing

The book of Genesis emphasizes the blessing of a father to his sons. The patriarchs Abraham, Isaac, and Jacob all gave formal blessings to their children—and, in Jacob's case, to some grandchildren. Receiving a blessing from one's father was a high honor, and losing a blessing was tantamount to a curse.

An Old Testament blessing of a father to his sons included words of encouragement, details regarding each son's inheritance, and prophetic words concerning the future. For example, Isaac's blessing on Jacob (which was meant for Esau) gave him the earth's bounty and authority over his brother (Genesis 27:28–29). It also promised that those who blessed Jacob would be blessed, and those who cursed him would receive a curse—words that echo God's promise to Abraham in Genesis 12:3. A patriarch's final blessing was important in biblical times as a practical matter of inheritance rights. In addition, some final blessings included prophetic statements that reveal God's supernatural power at work through the men of His choosing.

Chapter 7

TWELVE TRIBES, ONE DESTINY

"All these are the twelve tribes of Israel: and this is it that their father spake unto them, and blessed them; every one according to his blessing he blessed them." (Genesis 49:28, KJV)

The Children of Israel

In the Bible we often hear about the descendants of Jacob's sons referred to by the son's name—Gad, Zebulun, Issachar, and so on—but Joseph's descendants are referred to by the names of Joseph's two sons, Manasseh and Ephraim. An example of this would be in II Chronicles 30. The children (or tribes) of Israel in the Bible are the descendants of Jacob. The term "children of Israel" emphasizes the lineage of the Hebrew people as coming through the patriarch Jacob. The children of Israel are also called Israelites.

It all started with God's promise of a family—a big family—to a childless couple, Abraham and Sarah (Genesis 11:30; 12:1–3). God miraculously provided a son, Isaac, to fulfill the promise (Genesis 21:3), and He repeated the father's promise to the son (Genesis 21:12; 26:3–4). Isaac married Rebekah, and they were childless too, until God intervened and provided a son, Jacob, to continue the promise (Genesis 25:26). God then reaffirmed the Abrahamic Covenant with Jacob (Genesis 28:14–15). Later, God changed Jacob's name to Israel (Genesis 35:10). Jacob (Israel) had twelve sons who carried on the family line; each son's descendants formed a particular tribe of Israel, and all the descendants of Jacob were collectively called the children of Israel.

The Abrahamic Covenant

The Abrahamic covenant is an agreement between two parties. There are two basic types of covenants: conditional and unconditional. A conditional or bilateral covenant is an agreement that is binding on both parties for its fulfillment. Both parties agree to fulfill certain conditions. If either party fails to meet their responsibilities, the covenant is broken and neither party has to fulfill the expectations of the covenant. An unconditional or unilateral covenant is an agreement between two parties, but only one of the two parties has to do something. Nothing is required of the other party.

"Children of Israel" became the most common term for the Israelites in the Bible. Its use is a constant reminder of the faithfulness and power of God. The Lord who formed the nation of Israel has been faithful to keep His promises to the sons of Abraham, Isaac, and Jacob, and His great power has been on display throughout their history.

The Genealogy of the Tribes

Jacob, later called Israel, was the second-born son of Isaac and Rebecca, the younger twin brother of Esau, and the grandson of Abraham and Sarah. According to biblical texts, he was chosen by God to be the patriarch of the Israelite nation. From what is known of Jacob, he had two wives, the sisters Leah and Rachel, and two concubines, the sisters Bilhah and Zilpah, by whom he had at least thirteen children.

Though it is possible he may have had more sons and daughters than what is recorded in surviving texts, only twelve sons would form the basis for the twelve tribes of Israel: Reuben,

Simeon, Levi, Judah, Issachar, Zebulun, Joseph, Benjamin, Dan, Naphtali, Gad, and Asher. Jacob was known to display favoritism among his children, particularly for Joseph and Benjamin, the sons of his favorite wife, Rachel, and so the tribes themselves were not treated equally in a divine sense. Joseph, despite being the second-youngest son, received double the inheritance of his brothers, treated as if he were the firstborn son instead of Reuben, and so his tribe was later split into two tribes, named after his sons, Ephraim and Manasseh.

The Sons of Leah: Reuben, Simeon, Levi, Judah, Issachar, and Zebulun

Leah is an important figure in the Judeo-Christian tradition, the unloved wife of the biblical patriarch Jacob. Leah was Jacob's first wife, and the older sister of his second (and favored) wife Rachel. She is the mother of Jacob's first son Reuben. She had three more sons, namely Simeon, Levi, and Judah, but did not bear another son until Rachel offered her a night with Jacob in exchange for some mandrake root. These rooted plants contain hallucinogenic alkaloids, and the shape of their roots often resembles human figures; they have been associated with a variety of superstitious practices throughout history. They have long been used in magic rituals. Leah gave birth to two more sons after this, Issachar and Zebulun, and a daughter called Dinah.

The Sons of Rachel: Joseph and Benjamin

Rachel was a biblical figure, the favorite of Jacob's two wives, and the mother of Joseph and Benjamin. Rachel's father was Laban. Her older sister was Leah, Jacob's first wife. Her aunt Rebecca was Jacob's mother. The Bible first mentions Laban in Genesis 24:29. Laban was the brother of Isaac's wife, Rebekah. Laban was involved in the decision to allow his sister to travel to a foreign land and marry a man she had never met (Genesis 24:50, 55). Jacob returned to his mother's homeland and met Laban's daughter Rachel, with whom he fell madly in love (Genesis

29:18). Laban promised to give Rachel to Jacob if he would work for him for seven years (Genesis 29:19–20).

Laban continued to connive throughout his and Jacob's twenty-year relationship (Genesis 31:38). However, God blessed Jacob because Jacob was His choice to carry on the covenant He had made with his grandfather Abraham (Genesis 28:11–15). Genesis 31:1–3 indicates that Laban's sons were jealous of Jacob because of how much God had prospered him. They said, *"Jacob has taken everything our father owned and has gained all this wealth from what belonged to our father."* And Jacob noticed that Laban's attitude toward him was not what it had been. Then the Lord said to Jacob, *"Go back to the land of your fathers and to your relatives, and I will be with you."*

The Sons of Bilhah, Rachel's Handmaid: Dan and Naphtali

Bilhah is a woman mentioned in the Book of Genesis. Genesis 29:29 describes her as Laban's handmaid, who was given to Rachel to be her handmaid on Rachel's marriage to Jacob. When Rachel failed to have children, Rachel gave Bilhah to Jacob like a wife to bear him children. Bilhah gave birth to two sons, whom Rachel claimed as her own and named Dan and Naphtali. Genesis 35:22 expressly calls Bilhah Jacob's concubine (pilegesh).

The Sons of Zilpah, Leah's Handmaid: Gad and Asher

When Leah saw that she had stopped having children, she took her servant Zilpah and gave her to Jacob like a wife to bear him children as well.

Ephraim and Manasseh

Jacob elevated the descendants of Ephraim and Manasseh (the two sons of Joseph and his Egyptian wife Asenath) to the status of full tribes due to Joseph receiving a double portion after Reuben lost his birthright because of his transgression with Bilhah.

A House Divided from the Start

Throughout their history in the Promised Land, the children of Israel struggled with conflict among the tribes. The disunity went all the way back to the patriarch Jacob, who presided over a house divided. The sons of Leah and the sons of Rachel had their share of contention even in Jacob's lifetime (Genesis 37:1–11). The enmity among the half-brothers continued in the time of the judges. Benjamin (one of Rachel's tribes) took up arms against the other tribes (Judges 20). Israel's first king, Saul, was of the tribe of Benjamin. When David was crowned king—David was from the tribe of Judah (one of Leah's tribes)—the Benjamites rebelled (2 Samuel 2–3). After a long war (2 Samuel 3:1), David succeeded in uniting all twelve tribes (5:1–5).

The frailty of the union was exposed, however, when David's son Absalom promoted himself as the new king and removed many Israelites away from their allegiance to David (2 Samuel 15). Significantly, Absalom set up his throne in Hebron, the site of the former capital. A later revolt was led by a man named Sheba against David and the tribe of Judah (2 Samuel 20:1–2).

The reign of David's son Solomon saw more unrest when one of the king's servants, Jeroboam, rebelled. Jeroboam was on the king's errand when he met the prophet Ahijah, who told him that God was going to give him authority over ten of the twelve tribes of Israel. God's reason for the division of the kingdom was definitive: *"Because they have forsaken me . . . and have not walked in my ways."* However, God promised that David's dynasty would continue, albeit over a much smaller kingdom, for the sake of God's covenant with David and for the sake of Jerusalem, God's chosen city. When Solomon learned of the prophecy, he sought to kill Jeroboam, who fled to Egypt for sanctuary (1 Kings 11:26–40).

After Solomon's death, his son Rehoboam was set to become the next king. Jeroboam returned from Egypt and led a group of people to confront Rehoboam with a demand for a lighter tax burden. When Rehoboam refused the demand, ten of the tribes rejected Rehoboam and David's dynasty (1 Kings 12:16), and Ahijah's prophecy was fulfilled. Only Judah and Benjamin remained loyal to King Rehoboam. The northern tribes crowned Jeroboam as their king. Rehoboam made plans to mount an assault on the rebel tribes, but the Lord prevented him from taking that action. Meanwhile, Jeroboam further consolidated his power by instituting a form of calf worship unique to his kingdom and declaring that pilgrimages to Jerusalem were unnecessary. Thus, the people of the northern tribes would have no contact with the tribes of Judah and Benjamin.

"So Israel has been in rebellion against the house of David to this day" (1 Kings 12:19). From that point forward, the divided monarchy is identified distinctly in Scripture: the northern kingdom is called "Israel" (and at times "Ephraim"), while the southern kingdom is known as *"Judah."* From the divine perspective, this division was an act of judgment for covenant unfaithfulness—particularly the persistent sin of idolatry in violation of God's commands. From the human perspective, however, the rupture arose from tribal tension, political dissatisfaction, and leadership failure. The enduring principle is clear: sin produces division. Scripture consistently affirms this truth (1 Corinthians 1:13; 11:18; James 4:1), demonstrating that spiritual compromise inevitably fractures unity. The good news is that God, in His mercy, has promised a reuniting of the northern and southern kingdoms:

"He will raise a banner for the nations, gather the exiles of Israel; He will assemble the scattered people of Judah who are from the four quarters of the earth, Ephraim's jealousy will vanish, and Judah's enemies will be destroyed; Ephraim will not be jealous of Judah, nor Judah hostile toward Ephraim." (Isaiah 11:12–13)

When the Prince of Peace—Jesus Christ—reigns in His millennial kingdom, all hostility, jealousy, and conflict among the tribes will be put to rest.

The Tribes of Israel

Reuben (רְאוּבֵן Rə'ūḇēn)

The Book of Joshua records that the tribes of Reuben, Gad, and half of Manasseh were allocated land by Moses on the eastern side of the Jordan River and the Dead Sea (Joshua 13:15–23). The Tribe of Reuben was allocated the territory immediately east of the Dead Sea, reaching from the Arnon River in the south, and as far north as the Dead Sea stretched, with an eastern border vaguely defined by the land dissolving into desert; the territory included the plain of Madaba.

The territories described in Joshua 13 depict Gad as being to the north of Reuben, while the description in Numbers 32 and 34 has Reubenites living near Heshbon, surrounded by Gadites. The Bible (Book of Numbers) divides the tribe of Reuben into four clans or families: the Hanochites, Palluites, Hezronites, and Carmites, which according to the Bible were descended from Reuben's sons Hanoch, Pallu, Hazron, and Carmi.

Reuben lost his birthrights from Jacob because he was characterized as fickle, "unstable as water," and condemned to no longer have excellency in the family due to his crime of having sexual relations with his father's wife Bilhah. The tribes of Reuben and Gad requested they receive land in the territory east of Jordan, because it was suitable for their needs as livestock grazers. In exchange for their promise to help with the conquest of the land west of the Jordan, Moses accepted their request and granted to them and half of Manasseh land east of the Jordan. Following the death of Moses, Joshua became the leader of the Israelites, and with the help of these eastern tribes including Reuben, conquered some of Canaan and assigned the land of Israel to the various twelve tribes.

The Bible describes that after the conquest of the land under Joshua until the formation of the first Kingdom of Israel, the Tribe of Reuben was a part of a loose confederation of Israelite tribes. No central government existed, and in times of crisis the people were led by ad hoc leaders known as Judges. In this period Reuben declined to take part in the war against various nations, the people instead idly resting among their flocks as if it were a time of peace, though the decision to do so was taken with a heavy heart.

When the threat from the Philistines was mounting, the Israelite tribes decided to form a strong centralized monarchy to meet the challenge, and the Tribe of Reuben joined the new kingdom with Saul as the first king. After the death of Saul, all the tribes other than Judah remained loyal to the monarchy of Saul, but after the death of Ishbosheth, Saul's son and successor to the throne of Israel, the Tribe of Reuben joined the other northern Israelite tribes in making David, who was then the king of Judah, king of a reunited Kingdom of Israel.

According to the Book of Chronicles, several Reubenites aided David as members of his mighty warriors in conquering the City of David. Also, according to Chronicles, during the reign of King Saul, Reuben instigated a war with the Hagarites, and was victorious; in another portion of the same text, Reuben is said to have been assisted in this war by Gad and the eastern half of Manasseh. The Hagrites were associated with the Ishmaelites mentioned in the Bible, the inhabitants of the regions of Jetur, Naphish, and Nodab lying east of Gilead. Their name is understood to be related to that of the biblical Hagar. They lived a nomadic, animal-herding lifestyle in sparsely populated land east of the Israelites.

Simeon (שִׁמְעוֹן Šĭmə'ōn)

At its height, the territory occupied by the Tribe of Simeon was in the southwest of Canaan, bordered on the east and south by the tribe of Judah; the boundaries with the tribe of Judah are vague, and it seems that Simeon may have been an enclave within the west of the territory of the tribe of Judah. Historians depict Simeon as one of the less significant tribes in the Kingdom of Judah. In the opening words of the Book of Judges, following the death of Joshua, the Israelites "asked the Lord" which tribe should be first to go to occupy its allotted territory, and the tribe of Judah was identified as the first tribe. According to this narrative, the tribe of Judah invited the tribe of Simeon to fight with them in alliance to secure each of their allotted territories.

Jacob pronounced a curse upon the anger of Simeon and Levi, no doubt remembering when they treacherously and barbarously destroyed the Shechemites (son of Gilead), an act Jacob deeply resented for the barbarous way in which it was done and the reproach it brought upon his entire family (Genesis 34:24–30). Simeon's anger was evil, not because indignation against sin is unwarranted, but because his wrath was marked by deeds of fierceness and cruelty. Righteous anger and indignation, the kind Jesus exhibited in cleansing the temple, for example, is never characterized by cruelty. The swords of Simeon, which should have been only weapons of defense, were weapons of violence to do wrong to others, not to save themselves from wrong.

As Christians, we learn from the tribe of Simeon that anger is the cause of a great deal of sin when it is allowed to boil over without restraint, resulting in a scenario in which hurts are multiplied (Proverbs 29:11). Anger leaves devastation in its wake, often with irreparable consequences. Simeon and Levi appeared to be inseparable brothers who are often mentioned together in Scripture, an indication that, like many brothers and sisters, they may have "brought out the worst in each other." Christian parents who see this type of relationship developing in siblings whose influence upon one another is unhealthy, would do well to consider separating them from one another in circumstances where their unfortunate tendency to spur one another to wrong may exert itself.

Levi (לֵוִי Lēwī)

The Tribe of Levi is one of the tribes of Israel, traditionally descended from Levi, son of Jacob. The descendants of Aaron, who was the first "kohen gadol" (high priest) of Israel, were designated as the priestly class, the Kohanim. The Tribe of Levi served particular religious duties for the Israelites and had political responsibilities as well. In return, the landed tribes were expected to give tithes to the Kohanim, the priests working in the Temple in Jerusalem, particularly the tithe known as the Maaser Rishon. The Levites who were not Kohanim played music in the Temple or served as guards. When Joshua led the Israelites into the land of Canaan the Levites were the only Israelite tribe that received cities but were not allowed to be landowners, because "the Lord God of Israel is their inheritance, as he said to them" (Book of Joshua, Joshua 13:33).

The remaining Levites were divided into three groups: Gershonites (descended from Gershon), Kohathites (from Kohath), and Merarites (from Merari). Each division filled different roles in the Tabernacle and later in the Temple services. Levites' principal roles in the Temple included singing Psalms during Temple services, performing construction and maintenance for the Temple, serving as guards, and performing other services. Levites also served as teachers and judges, maintaining Cities of Refuge in biblical times. The Book of Ezra reports that the Levites were responsible for the construction of the Second Temple and translated and explained the Torah when it was publicly read.

During the Exodus the Levite tribe were particularly zealous in protecting the Mosaic law in the face of those worshipping the golden calf, which may have been a reason for their priestly status. Although the Levites were not counted in the census among the children of Israel, they were numbered separately as a special army. Levi was the third-born, and his mother was Jacob's wife Leah. Levi and each of his eleven brothers became the heads of the twelve tribes of Israel. The Bible does not give many details of Levi's life; however, in Genesis 34, Levi and his brother Simeon defend the honor of their sister, Dinah, although the manner in which they went about it was appalling.

This is what happened: when Dinah was away from her father's house one day, she was raped by Shechem, the son of the Hivite ruler of that territory. When Dinah's brothers heard about the rape, they were furious. Shechem, who desired Dinah as his wife, asked for Dinah's hand, so Dinah's brothers tricked him and said that first he, his father, and the other men of the city must be circumcised. Shechem and his father agreed, and all the males went through the rite of circumcision. But three days later, when the men of Shechem were still in pain, Levi and Simeon strapped on their swords and attacked the city, killing every man and plundering the city. Jacob was angry at Levi and Simeon because of their murderous attack, but Levi and Simeon were unapologetic.

Levi was also involved in selling his brother Joseph to merchants who sold Joseph as a slave in Egypt. Joseph's brothers were jealous of him, for their father showed him much favoritism. Joseph went through several hard years in Egypt but eventually became second-in-command to Pharaoh due to his faithfulness and the Lord's blessing (Genesis 41:39–41).

Later, Joseph's brothers, including Levi, were forced to come buy food from Egypt, and it was during one of their trips there they discovered the man they'd been dealing with for food was their brother Joseph. The brothers begged forgiveness from Joseph with true repentance, and Joseph forgave them. Eventually, Joseph brought his whole family to live in Egypt.

Before Jacob died in Egypt, he called his sons to him and spoke words of prophecy over each of them. He said this of Levi: *"Simeon and Levi are brothers—their swords are weapons of violence. Let me not enter their council, let me not join their assembly, for they have killed men in their anger and hamstrung oxen as they pleased. Cursed be their anger, so fierce, and their fury, so cruel! I will scatter them in Jacob and disperse them in Israel"* (Genesis 49:5–7). Jacob's harsh words showed that Levi and Simeon's bloody vengeance for their sister's rape had lasting consequences. The descendants of Levi became numerous, but they were indeed scattered throughout the Promised Land. Moses was a descendant of Levi (Exodus 2:1). Other notable men of Levi's family line were Eli, Ezra, and John the Baptist.

Judah (יְהוּדָה Yəhūdā)

Judah's second-to-youngest brother, Joseph, was preferred by their father, and Judah and his brothers hated Joseph (Genesis 37:3–4). One day, the brothers threw Joseph in a cistern and conspired to kill him. The eldest sibling, Reuben, argued against this course of action, intending to rescue Joseph from the others (verses 21–22). But while the brothers ate lunch, and in Reuben's absence, a caravan approached, and Judah came up with a plan to sell Joseph to the caravan's merchants as a slave (verses 26–27). The brothers agreed, and Joseph was sold and taken to Egypt.

It is possible that Judah felt remorse or guilt for his actions, for *"at that time, Judah left his brothers and went down to stay with a man from the city of Adullam named Hirah"* (Genesis 38:1). There, Judah married a Canaanite woman who gave Judah three sons: Er, Onan, and Shelah. When Er grew up, Judah gave him a wife named Tamar; however, Er was an evil man, so the Lord put him to death (verse 7). Following the custom of Levirate marriage, Tamar was then given to Onan, who selfishly refused to give Tamar children (verse 9); he was also put to death by the Lord for his actions. Shelah was too young to take a wife, so Judah ordered Tamar to live as a widow in her father's house (verse 11).

After several years Judah's own wife died, and he grieved. When he recovered, he traveled to Timnah to oversee the shearing of his sheep. Tamar, still a widow although Shelah had grown up, heard that her father-in-law was coming, and she devised a plan. Tamar put on a veil and pretended to be a prostitute on the road to Timnah (Genesis 38:14). The veil hid her identity from Judah, and Judah slept with her. Tamar became pregnant, which had been her goal all along.

Three months later, when Judah found out that his supposedly chaste daughter-in-law was pregnant, he was filled with rage: *"Bring her out and have her burned to death!"* he demanded (verse 24). As she was being brought out for punishment as a harlot, Tamar produced evidence that her pregnancy was due to Judah's own immorality. Judah saw his hypocrisy and repented, saying, *"She is more righteous than I, since I wouldn't give her to my son Shelah"* (verse 26). Judah did not have sexual relations with Tamar after that. She later gave birth to twins, two boys named Perez and Zerah (verses 29–30).

Meanwhile, God was with Judah's brother Joseph in Egypt, elevating Joseph to a place of power second only to the Pharaoh himself (Genesis 41:39–40). Joseph had interpreted the king's dream warning of seven years of plenty followed by seven years of famine, and so Pharaoh put Joseph in charge of gathering grain to store for the lean years. Under Joseph's supervision, a large amount of grain was set aside (verse 49). When the great famine came upon the land, it affected even Canaan. Judah and his brothers traveled from Canaan to Egypt to buy some of the surplus food. Joseph eventually revealed himself to his brothers, who were remorseful for what they had done to him (for more on this, see Genesis 42–45).

Soon, Joseph brought his entire family to the land of Egypt, where their descendants would live for several hundred years, according to God's great plan for His people. This is where Jacob died, and before he passed, he called all his sons to bless them. Despite all Judah's faults, his blessing from Jacob was both rich and wonderful; in it, Jacob foretold that Judah's house would be the greatest, and the scepter, or rule, would not depart from his descendants (see Genesis 49:8–12 for the full blessing). Jacob's words held true, for, many years later, Judah's line produced King David and his dynasty and, eventually, through the line of Perez, came the Messiah, Jesus Christ, who is called *"the Lion of the tribe of Judah"* (Revelation 5:5).

The Lion of the tribe of Judah is a symbol found in Genesis and Revelation. In Genesis, Jacob blesses his son Judah, referring to him and his future tribe as a lion's cub and a lion (Genesis 49:9). In Revelation, this symbol is seen again when the Lion of the tribe of Judah is declared to have triumphed and is worthy to open the scroll and its seven seals (Revelation 5:5). Jesus is the One who is worthy to open the scroll (see John 5:22). Therefore, Jesus is the Lion of the tribe of Judah.

Dan (דָּן Dān)

Dan was the fifth of twelve sons born to the Jewish patriarch Jacob. Dan's mother was Bilhah, Rachel's maidservant. Dan's younger brother was Naphtali. The account of Dan's birth is contained in Genesis 30:1–8. Rachel, who had remained childless, was envious of her sister, Leah, who had already given birth to four sons of Jacob. Barrenness held great shame for women in ancient cultures, so Rachel followed the custom of the day and presented her maidservant, Bilhah, to Jacob as a third wife. When Bilhah gave birth to Dan, Rachel considered the child her own. Rachel named him Dan, meaning *"he judged,"* because she felt that God had judged and vindicated her through the child's birth.

Dan had only one son, Hushim, to carry on his bloodline (Genesis 46:23). He is listed as Shuham in Numbers 26:42 and identified as the ancestor of the clan of the Shuhamites. Some of Dan's descendants are mentioned in the days of the wilderness wanderings. Oholiab was a skilled craftsman appointed by God to work on the tabernacle (Exodus 31:6; 35:34; 38:23). An unnamed son whose father was Egyptian and whose mother was from the tribe of Dan blasphemed the name of the Lord and was put to death (Leviticus 24:10–11). Ahiezer was a leader of the tribe of Dan (Numbers 1:12; 2:25; 7:66–71; 10:25).

When Israel entered the Promised Land, the tribe that descended from Dan was allotted a portion of Canaan between Judah and Ephraim bordering the Mediterranean coast (Joshua 19:40–48). However, except for the valley of Zorah and Eshtaol, Dan's tribe failed to gain control of the territory, especially after the Philistines settled there. In the book of Judges, Samson, who was from the tribe of Dan, was called by God to fight against the Philistines (Judges 13–16). Eventually, Dan's tribe migrated to the north and seized the city of Laish. They renamed the city Dan and took up residence in the surrounding areas (Judges 18).

In Moses' blessing, Dan's tribe is called *"a lion's cub, springing out of Bashan"* (Deuteronomy 33:22). Some believe the reference relates to Dan's northern migration and capture of Laish. After Dan resettled to the north, the tribe became associated with idolatry (Judges 18:30–31; 2 Kings 10:29).

Naphtali (נַפְתָּלִי Naptālī)

Israel's tribes were named for Jacob's children. Naphtali, being the sixth son of Jacob, is one of Israel's twelve tribes. In the time of Moses, Naphtali was divided into four clans: the Jahzeelites, the Gunites, the Jezerites, and the Shillemites, named after Naphtali's sons (Numbers 26:48–49). Naphtali was borne by Rachel's maidservant, Bilhah. He was her second and last child with Jacob. When Naphtali was born, Rachel said, *"I have had a great struggle with my sister, and I have won"* (Genesis 30:8). Naphtali means *"my struggle."*

Naphtali was one of six tribes chosen to stand on Mount Ebal and pronounce curses (Deuteronomy 27:13). By means of these curses, the people promised God they would refrain from certain behaviors. For example, one curse says, "Cursed is the man who moves his neighbor's boundary stone" (Deuteronomy 27:17). Another states, *"Cursed is the man who withholds justice from the alien or fatherless or the widow"* (Deuteronomy 27:19). Still another: *"Cursed is the man who kills his neighbor secretly"* (Deuteronomy 27:24). In all, Naphtali helped deliver twelve such admonishments (Deuteronomy 27:15–26).

When Jacob blessed his twelve sons, he said, *"Naphtali is a doe set free that bears beautiful fawns"* (Genesis 49:21). The image presented is of one who springs forth with great speed and provides good news. Later, Moses blessed the tribe: *"Naphtali is abounding with the favor of the Lord and is full of his blessing; he will inherit southward to the lake"* (Deuteronomy 33:23). In Joshua 19:32–39, we learn that Naphtali's land was in northern Israel, bordering Asher's territory, and the Sea of Kinnereth (or Galilee) touched the southern portion of its territory.

Despite all their blessings, the tribe of Naphtali failed to obey God's command to drive out all the Canaanites living in their territory. Therefore, *"the Naphtalites too lived among the Canaanite inhabitants of the land, and those living in Beth Shemesh or Beth Anath became forced labor for them"* (Judges 1:33). In Judges 4:6–9, we learn that Barak was a Naphtalite. He had been chosen by God to lead a military force of 10,000 of his tribe against their Canaanite oppressors. However, when the time came for action, Barak responded in fear and cowardice, agreeing to fight against King Jabin's army only if Deborah the judge would accompany him. Deborah consented, but she prophesied that the honor for the victory would go to a woman and not to Barak. The prophecy was fulfilled in Judges 4:17–22.

"The Song of Deborah and Barak" (Judges 5) relates that the tribe of Naphtali risked their lives *"on the heights of the field"* (verse 18) and so was honored in the victory over the Canaanites. Later, Naphtali responded to Gideon's call to repel the Midianites, Amalekites, and others from the East from their encampment in the Jezreel Valley (Judges 6:35). Along with the tribes of Asher and Manasseh, Naphtali followed Gideon into battle and chased the Midianites to Zererah and Abel Meholah (Judges 7:23).

When the time came for David to assume the throne, the tribe of Naphtali provided "1,000 officers, together with 37,000 men carrying shields and spears," along with a caravan of food, to help him (1 Chronicles 12:34, 40). When King Solomon was building the temple, he hired Huram, a man whose mother was a Naphtalite, to do the bronze work (1 Kings 7:13–47).

In the time of Christ, the land of Naphtali was part of the area of Galilee, and it was viewed by the Jews in Judea as a place of dishonor, full of Gentile pagans (see John 1:46; 7:52). But Isaiah had prophesied that Naphtali would be honored: *"In the past he humbled . . . the land of Naphtali, but in the future he will honor Galilee of the Gentiles, by the way of the sea, along the Jordan"* (Isaiah 9:1). This honor came with the coming of Jesus Christ. All Jesus' disciples but Judas, who betrayed Him, hailed from Galilee, and much of Jesus' ministry took place there. Thus, *"on those living in the land of the shadow of death a light has dawned"* (Isaiah 9:2).

The tribe of Naphtali had its ups and downs. Its history includes incomplete obedience and shades of cowardice, but it also includes bravery under Gideon and a godly support of King David. Probably the greatest lesson we can take from Naphtali is that God exalts the humble. Naphtali (as part of Galilee) was despised, and Nazareth was the lowest of the low. Yet Nazareth was Jesus' hometown, and Galilee was exactly where Jesus chose to begin His ministry. For our sakes, He became *"despised and rejected by men"* (Isaiah 53:3). The King of kings had the most unpretentious start. He is truly "humble in heart" (Matthew 11:29).

Gad (גָּד Gāḏ)

Israel's 12 tribes, of which Gad was one, were named for Jacob's children (or grandchildren, in the cases of Ephraim and Manasseh). *"Israel"* was God's name for Jacob (Genesis 32:22–30); therefore, the phrase *"children of Israel"* is a way of referring to Jacob's descendants. Jacob's son Gad was born in Paddan Aram to Jacob's first wife's maidservant, Zilpah (Genesis 35:26). When Jacob blessed his 12 sons, he said, *"Gad will be attacked by a band of raiders, but he will attack them at their heels"* (Genesis 49:19). Later, Moses blessed the tribe of Gad, saying, *"Blessed is he who enlarges Gad's domain! Gad lives there like a lion, tearing at arm or head. He chose the best land for himself; the leader's portion was kept for him. When the heads of the people assembled, he carried out the LORD's righteous will, and his judgments concerning Israel"* (Deuteronomy 33:20–21).

The tribe of Gad was one of three (Reuben and the half-tribe of Manasseh were the others) to fight for and be awarded lands east of the Jordan River, the gateway to the Promised Land (Joshua 12:6; 13:8–13). When Gad and the other tribes first requested this land outside of the Promised Land, Moses warned that their actions could discourage the others from taking the land God had given, much like the ten spies' fearful report forty years previously. The Reubenites and Gadites said, *"We would like to build pens here for our livestock and cities for our women and children. But we will arm ourselves for battle and go ahead of the Israelites until we have brought them to their place. Meanwhile our women and children will live in fortified cities, for protection from the inhabitants of the land. We will not return to our homes until each of the Israelites has received their inheritance. We will not receive any inheritance with them on the other side of the Jordan, because our inheritance has come to us on the east side of the Jordan"* (Numbers 32:16–19).

Moses agreed: *"Then Moses said to them, 'If you will do this—if you will arm yourselves before the LORD for battle and if all of you who are armed cross over the Jordan before the LORD until he has driven his enemies out before him—then when the land is subdued before the LORD, you may return and be free from your obligation to the LORD and to Israel. And this land will be your possession before the LORD. But if you fail to do this, you will be sinning against the LORD; and you may be sure that your sin will find you out'"* (Numbers 32:20–23).

The tribes were faithful to their commitment (Numbers 32:25; Joshua 22:1–6). When they returned to their own land, they built an altar. The other Israelites came out against them, thinking they were rebelling against the Lord. But the tribes of Gad, Reuben, and the half-tribe of Manasseh called on the Lord saying He knew their motives and if they had acted in rebellion or disobedience they should not be spared. In fact, they had built the altar not to make sacrifices but *"to be a witness between us and you and the generations that follow, that we will worship the LORD at his sanctuary with our burnt offerings, sacrifices and fellowship offerings. Then in the future your descendants will not be able to say to ours, 'You have no share in the LORD'"* (Joshua 22:27).

Though the tribes had settled on the other side of the Jordan, they were still very much committed to worshipping God. They were still part of Israel and wanted to prevent the Jordan River, a significant geographical divide between Gad and the majority of the other tribes, from spiritually dividing God's people then or in future generations (Joshua 22:10–34). *"And the Reubenites and Gadites gave the altar this name: A Witness Between Us—that the LORD is God"* (Joshua 22:34).

Gad, along with all the other northern tribes of Israel, was sent into exile in 722 BC (2 Kings 15:29–17:41). Gad's specific circumstances, seemingly triggered by the half-tribe of Manasseh's unfaithfulness to God, are described in 1 Chronicles 5:11–26. We see in the tribe of Gad fidelity to God and to their commitments to others. Perhaps the most important lesson we learn from Gad (and all the other tribes) is to recognize the need for complete faith and trust in God. God commanded Moses to remind the Israelites to *"carefully follow the terms of this covenant, so that you may prosper in everything you do"* (Deuteronomy 29:9). *"Make sure there is no man or woman, clan or tribe among you today whose heart turns away from the Lord our God to go and worship the gods of those nations; make sure there is no root among you that produces such bitter poison"* (Deuteronomy 29:18).

Asher (אָשֵׁר ʻĀšēr)

Asher is one of Israel's twelve tribes. In the time of Moses, Asher was divided into five clans: the Imnites; the Ishvites; and the Berites; and, through Beriah, the Berite patriarch, two more clans: the Heberites and the Malkielites. The first three clans were named after Asher's sons; the fourth and fifth after Beriah's sons (Numbers 26:44–45). Asher was Jacob's eighth son. His mother was Leah's maidservant, Zilpah, and he was her second and last child with Jacob. When Asher was born, Leah said, *"How happy am I! The women will call me happy"* (Genesis 30:13). Asher's name means "happy."

Asher was one of six tribes chosen to stand on Mount Ebal and pronounce curses (Deuteronomy 27:13). Through these curses, the people promised God they would refrain from bad behavior. For example, one curse says, *"Cursed is the man who dishonors his father or his mother"* (Deuteronomy 27:16). Another states, *"Cursed is the man who leads the blind astray on the road"* (Deuteronomy 27:18). Still another: *"Cursed is the man who sleeps with his mother-in-law"* (Deuteronomy 27:23). In all, Asher delivered twelve admonishments (Deuteronomy 27:15–26).

When Jacob blessed his sons, he said, *"Asher's food will be rich; he will provide delicacies fit for a king"* (Genesis 49:20). Later, Moses blessed the tribe, saying, *"Most blessed of the sons is*

Asher; let him be favored by his brothers, and let him bathe his feet in oil. The bolts of your gates will be iron and bronze, and your strength will equal your days" (Deuteronomy 33:24). Washing one's feet in oil was a sign of prosperity, and Jacob's reference to Asher's food being "rich" indicated that Asher would possess fertile lands. In Joshua 19:24–31, we learn that Asher received land along the Mediterranean coast.

Despite all its blessings, the tribe of Asher failed to drive out the Canaanites, and *"because of this the people of Asher lived among the Canaanite inhabitants of the land"* (Judges 1:31–32). In the time of Deborah and Barak, *"Asher remained on the coast and stayed in its coves"* rather than join the fight against Jabin, a Canaanite king (Judges 5:17). This failure to aid their fellow tribes could indicate a lack of reliance on God, a lack of effort, a fear of the enemy, or a reluctance to upset those with whom they did business. Thus, the example set here is a negative one: although Asher was richly blessed, they did not behave admirably; when the time for action came, they failed to trust in God and honor His plan.

Later in Judges, Asher does respond to Gideon's call to repel the Midianites, Amalekites, and others from the East (Judges 6:35). In another important gesture, Asher accepts Hezekiah's invitation to the tribes from the Northern Kingdom to join the Passover celebration in Jerusalem (2 Chronicles 30:11). This was considered an act of humility, proof of a contrite heart before God.

In the end, we find that Asher received many great blessings from God. Having received a blessing, they were expected to obey the Lord's commands. In this they sometimes succeeded and sometimes failed. We, too, have been blessed by God (Ephesians 1:3), and the Lord expects us to obey His commands (John 14:15). Just as Asher received a prophetic blessing from Jacob, God's children have been told, *"In his great mercy [God] has given us new birth into a living hope through the resurrection of Jesus Christ from the dead, and into an inheritance that can never perish, spoil or fade. This inheritance is kept in heaven for you, who through faith are shielded by God's power until the coming of the salvation that is ready to be revealed in the last time"* (1 Peter 1:3–5). Praise the Lord for His wonderful plans for us. What a comfort!

Issachar (יִשָּׂשכָר Yīssāškār)

Each of the twelve sons of Israel/Jacob received a blessing from his father just before Jacob's death. The twelve sons were the progenitors of the twelve tribes of Israel, and Jacob's blessings contained prophetic information about each tribe. In the case of the tribe of Issachar, Jacob prophesied, *"Issachar is a rawboned donkey, lying down between two burdens; He saw that rest was good, and that the land was pleasant; He bowed his shoulder to bear a burden, and became a band of slaves"* (Genesis 49:14–15).

The first part of the prophecy about the tribe of Issachar, whose name means either "he will bring a reward" or "man of wages," is somewhat obscure. The word translated "rawboned" in the NIV is translated "strong" in other versions. It can also mean "bony" as in "nothing but skin and bones." Therefore, the prophecy could either mean that the descendants of Issachar would be strong and robust, able to bear burdens, or that they would be thin and weak and unable to do so.

The image of a donkey lying down between its burdens can also be interpreted two ways. On one hand, it could portray a sturdy animal resting for the task ahead. On the other hand, donkeys also are known to stubbornly crouch between their burdens to keep from having to do the work. Again, the prophecy eludes a dogmatic interpretation. The subsequent history of Issachar in the Bible does not conclusively favor either construal.

As for the second part of the prophecy, some commentators believe it is an indication that the descendants of Issachar would be farmers—the reference to "a band of slaves" means they would be servants of the land. Others see it as a prediction of forced labor, although nothing in

Scripture indicates that the tribe of Issachar was ever forced into slavery of any kind. In fact, the Hebrew wording is so obscure that English translations vary widely. Consider the following:

King James Version (KJV): *"Issachar is a strong ass couching down between two burdens: And he saw that rest was good, and the land that it was pleasant; and bowed his shoulder to bear, and became a servant unto tribute."*

English Standard Version (ESV): *"Issachar is a strong donkey, crouching between the sheepfolds. He saw that a resting place was good, and that the land was pleasant, so he bowed his shoulder to bear, and became a servant at forced labor."*

New American Standard Bible (NASB): *"Issachar is a strong donkey, Lying down between the sheepfolds. When he saw that a resting place was good. And that the land was pleasant, He bowed his shoulder to bear burdens, And became a slave at forced labor."*

New International Version (NIV): *"Issachar is a rawboned donkey lying down between two saddlebags. When he sees how good is his resting place and how pleasant is his land, he will bend his shoulder to the burden and submit to forced labor."*

There is another reference to the men of Issachar during the time of David's struggle against Saul (1 Chronicles 12:32). The two hundred chiefs of Issachar who are faithful to David are described as those who "understood the times and knew what Israel should do." Scholars are divided on the meaning of the phrase *"understood the times."* Some portray the men of Issachar as politically astute, knowing how to use current events to their own advantage. Others interpret the phrase to mean they were known for their understanding of astronomy and physical science. Still others see them as men of prudence and wisdom who, because of their religious scholarship, knew that this was the proper time for David to become king. The truth is that we really don't know for sure.

As part of the Northern Kingdom of Israel, the territory of Issachar was conquered by the Assyrians around 720 BC and the tribe exiled. After that, all explicit biblical references to the tribe cease.

How are we to understand these references to Issachar and their different interpretations, and what do they mean to us as Christians? First, it's important to understand that Jacob's prophecies to his sons were just that—prophecies to his sons. We should be very careful when applying Old Testament passages to the Church Age or to Christians in general. We can, however, glean certain general principles regarding work and its rewards. The Bible makes it clear that work is a gift from God for the benefit of His people (Ecclesiastes 3:12–13; 5:18–20) and those who don't work shouldn't eat (2 Thessalonians 3:10). The Bible contains numerous references to those who work as reaping rewards, both in the temporal and spiritual realms (2 Chronicles 15:7; 1 Corinthians 3:8, 14; 2 John 1:8; Revelation 2:23; 22:12).

There are some who would point to the different translations of Genesis 49:14–15 as evidence of the unreliability of the Bible. However, it must be remembered that such cases of obscurity are extremely rare, and none of the cardinal doctrines of the Christian faith are ever in question. Whether the donkey was bony or robust does not affect the Bible's teaching on sin, death, judgment, heaven, hell, the atonement of Christ, or a myriad other doctrine. Scripture contains ample information regarding these doctrines to make them clearly understood to all who have *"ears to hear"* (Mark 4:9, 23).

Zebulun (זְבוּלֻן Zəḇūlun)

Zebulun is one of Israel's twelve tribes. In the time of Moses, Zebulun was divided into three clans: the Seredites, the Elonites, and the Jahleelites, named after Zebulun's sons (Numbers

26:26). The tribes were named for Jacob's children (or grandchildren, in the cases of Ephraim and Manasseh).

Jacob's tenth son, Zebulun, was the youngest of six sons borne by Leah. When Zebulun was born, Leah said, *"God has presented me with a precious gift. This time my husband will treat me with honor, because I have borne him six sons"* (Genesis 30:20). Zebulun means "dwelling" or "honor."

Zebulun was one of six tribes chosen to stand on Mount Ebal and pronounce curses (Deuteronomy 27:13). By means of these curses, the people promised God they would refrain from certain behaviors. For example, one curse says, *"Cursed is the man who carves an image or casts an idol—a thing detestable to the Lord"* (Deuteronomy 27:15). Another states, *"Cursed is the man who withholds justice from the alien, the fatherless or the widow"* (Deuteronomy 27:19). Still another: "Cursed is the man who does not uphold the words of this law by carrying them out (Deuteronomy 27:26). In all, Zebulun helped deliver twelve admonishments of this sort (Deuteronomy 27:15–26).

Upon entering the Promised Land, Zebulun failed to drive out the Canaanites living in Kitron and Nahalol, although Zebulun did subject them to forced labor (Judges 1:30). This was incomplete obedience to God's clear command to drive out all the inhabitants of the land (Numbers 33:52). Not responding fully to God's Word, as Zebulun demonstrated, is a trait to which we all can relate. How often do we choose to follow our own paths for various reasons, many of which may not be in concert with God's wishes?

Later, Zebulun returned to God and followed His commands. They participated in the battles led by Deborah and Barak, and they fought valiantly (Judges 4:6; 5:18). The judge Elon was a Zebulunite (Judges 12:11). During the kingdom years, Zebulun joined David at Hebron to transfer Saul's kingdom to David (1 Chronicles 12:23, 33, 40). This, too, provides insight into our behavior. While at times we turn away from God, His love for us, and ours for Him, draws us back into communion with Him and compliance with His will.

Zebulun's territory was located in what later became known as Galilee, in Northern Israel. Moses' blessing on the tribe was that they would prosper in their overseas dealings with Gentile nations (Deuteronomy 33:18–19). Isaiah prophesied, *"In the past [God] humbled the land of Zebulun . . . but in the future he will honor Galilee"* (Isaiah 9:1). Isaiah's prediction is Messianic: Galilee (including Zebulun) would be honored as the first to hear Christ's preaching, and this would more than compensate for their humiliation at the hands of the Assyrians centuries before.

Numerous verses in the Bible, especially in the Psalms, extol God for His unfailing patience, love, and faithfulness. Indirectly, Zebulun's history reminds us that God is always present when we return to Him. No matter how battered or bruised we may be or how ashamed we may feel about past transgressions, God can still use us.

Joseph (יוֹסֵף Yōsēp), Ephraim, and Manasseh

Joseph married Asenath who is a minor figure in the Book of Genesis. Asenath was a high-born, aristocratic Egyptian woman. She was the wife of Joseph and the mother of his sons, Manasseh and Ephraim. There are two Rabbinic approaches to Asenath: One holds that she was an ethnic Egyptian woman that converted to marry Joseph. This view has her accepting the Lord before marriage and then raising her two sons in the tenets of Judaism. This presents her as a positive example of conversion, and places her among the devout women converts.

The other approach argues she was not Egyptian by descent but was from the family of Jacob. Traditions that trace her to the family of Jacob relate that she was born as the daughter of Dinah. Dinah was raped by Shechem, and supposedly impregnated. Dinah left Asenath on the wall of Egypt, where she was later found by Potiphar. She was then raised by Potiphar and he married

with her. She is the same person with Zuleikha (Potiphar's wife). After Joseph became the

Pharaoh's chief assistant, he forgave her, and they got married.

Ephraim (אֶפְרַיִם ʻEp̄rayīm)

Israel's twelve tribes were named for Jacob's children or, in the case of Ephraim (and

Manasseh), his grandchildren. Ephraim was born in Egypt to Joseph's wife, Asenath. Joseph

named his second-born son "Ephraim" because *"God has made me fruitful in the land of my*

suffering" (Genesis 41:52). When Jacob gave his blessing to his grandsons Ephraim and

Manasseh, he chose to bless the younger Ephraim first, despite Joseph's protests. In doing so,

Jacob noted that Ephraim would be greater than Manasseh (Genesis 48:5–21).

Throughout the Old Testament, the name Ephraim often refers to the ten tribes comprising

Israel's Northern Kingdom, not just the single tribe named after Joseph's son (Ezekiel 37:16;

Hosea 5:3). The Northern Kingdom, also referred to as *"Israel,"* was taken into captivity by the

Assyrians in 722 BC (Jeremiah 7). The Southern Kingdom, also known as Judah, was conquered

by the Babylonians nearly 140 years later (586 BC). We learn from the tribe of Ephraim (and the

other tribes) about our human essence, who we are as people. The history of the early Israelites

reflects our universally flawed and sinful nature. As the book of Romans says, *"All have sinned*

and fall short of the glory of God" (Romans 3:23).

There are several specific events regarding the tribe of Ephraim that we can learn from.

While God gifted the tribe as warriors and valiant fighters (1 Chronicles 12:30), Ephraim failed to

follow God's order to remove the Canaanites from the Promised Land (Exodus 23:23–25; Judges

1:29; Joshua 16:10). During the time of the judges, the Ephraimites became angry with Gideon

because he had not initially called for their help in battling the Midianites (Judges 8:1). Gideon wisely displayed godly kindness and extolled the tribe's commitment and willingness to serve the Lord, thus diffusing what could have become an ugly situation (Judges 8:2–3).

However, ugliness did arise later, and again it can be linked to Ephraim's pride, jealousy, and self-centeredness. When Jephthah chose to fight (and defeat) the Ammonites without the aid of the proud Ephraim warriors, a civil war erupted, and 42,000 warriors from Ephraim were killed. As Jesus said in His Sermon on the Mount, we are to seek first the kingdom of God (Matthew 6:33). Do not seek glory for yourself; all honor and glory always belong to God, not to man.

Often, God chooses to use us in a manner less glamorous or spectacular than we would like. Do we pout? Do we yearn for glory? Do we control our pride and jealousy and accept God's will? Many of us, like the Ephraimites, have difficulty learning those lessons well. God says that we should accept what happens to us as His will, regardless of how good or bad those circumstances seem to us (1 Thessalonians 5:16–18).

Other lessons of Ephraim complete the picture of the wide range of human behavior. We see Ephraim turning away from God and doing wicked things (Isaiah 28:1–3), yet we also find the tribe recognizing the need to repent and obey by following the prophet Oded's instructions (2 Chronicles 28:12). The biggest lesson from the history of Ephraim is that God loves us as the Perfect Father despite our failings. He is patient and merciful beyond our understanding. He hears our cries of anguish, disciplines and guides us, knows our moments of repentance, and yearns for us to be in perfect communion with Him (Jeremiah 30:22; 31:18–20).

Manasseh (מְנַשֶּׁה Mənašše)

Israel's twelve tribes were named for Jacob's children or, in the case of Manasseh (and Ephraim), his grandchildren. After Jacob wrestled with Him all night, God renamed Jacob

"Israel," which means *"you have struggled with God and men and have overcome"* (Genesis 32:22–30). The name Israel represents not only the modern-day country but also, originally, Jacob's offspring to whom God promised a great nation whose *"descendants will be like dust of the earth . . . spread out to the west and to the east, to the north and to the south"* (Genesis 28:14).

Jacob's grandson, for whom the tribe was named, was born in Egypt to Joseph and his wife, Asenath, daughter of the priest Potiphera. Joseph named his firstborn *"Manasseh"* because God had made him "forget all my trouble and all my father's household" (Genesis 41:51).

This tribe provides us with many lessons; chief among them are messages about free will, obedience, faith, and the nature of God. Early on, we learn that Manasseh is frequently referred to as the "half-tribe" of Manasseh. This designation highlights the choice made by some of the tribe to reside east of the River Jordan (Numbers 32:33; Joshua 13:29–31). They believed the Transjordan was the more suitable land to raise their flocks. The rest of the tribe settled west of the Jordan, in Canaan, following Joshua's command to enter and possess the Promised Land. As is evident throughout Scripture, God endows His children with the freedom to choose.

Exercising free will can lead to undesirable or even disastrous results, especially if we disobey God or make selfish choices. Manasseh learned this lesson—painfully—when they failed to obey God's command to destroy the Canaanites. Part of this failure was due to a lack of faith that God would give them strength to overcome a seemingly unconquerable foe. Manasseh illustrates other human failings as well, such as greed and covetousness. The (half) tribe of Manasseh desired more land because they were "a numerous people." They may have had the numbers, but they were unwilling to follow Joshua's exhortation to clear *"the land of the Perizzites and Rephaites"* (Joshua 17:12–18).

On the other hand, the tribe of Manasseh at times exhibits faithfulness to God. Gideon, who would later become one of Israel's best judges, questioned God when called to *"save Israel out of Midian's hand."* One of Gideon's objections was that his *"clan is the weakest in Manasseh, and I am the least in my family"* (Judges 6:15). Gideon required proof from God—twice—before he acted (Judges 6:36–40). Once convinced of God's will, Gideon moved forward with 32,000 troops to conquer the Midianites. But then God told Gideon that he had too many troops for the job, and God reduced his corps to a mere 300 men. Following God's lead, this paltry force routed the enemy. The battle proved God was with Gideon and the half-tribe of Manasseh.

Other interesting lessons emerge. One is that God is just. Zelophehad, great-great-grandson of Manasseh, had no sons and died in the desert before entering the Promised Land. His daughters petitioned Moses, asking that the practice of male inheritance be changed so they could receive their deceased father's property. After consulting with the Lord, Moses agreed and developed rules designed to keep property within a family (Numbers 27:1–11).

[Note: The tribal account of Benjamin and the remaining material from Part VII will be completed in the next chapter delivery, Chapter 8: "A Family Scattered: The Tribes in History."]

Chapter 8

A FAMILY SCATTERED: THE TRIBES IN HISTORY

"In those days there was no king in Israel: every man did that which was right in his own eyes." (Judges 21:25, KJV)

In the previous chapter, we walked through the blessings spoken over each of Jacob's twelve sons and traced the significance of their tribal identities from the patriarchal tents to the allotted territories of the Promised Land. But a question remains that every serious student of Scripture must eventually confront: What happened next? What became of these tribes as the centuries rolled on, as kingdoms rose and crumbled, as foreign armies swept through the land, and as the people God had chosen for a purpose found themselves scattered across the ancient world?

The story of the tribes after their settlement in Canaan is not a tidy one. It is a story of faithfulness and failure, of worship and idolatry, of unity and devastating division. It is a story that includes one of the most despised people groups in biblical history, the Samaritans, and a long procession of kings, most of whom led God's people further away from the covenant that had defined them. And yet, through all of it, God's purposes were never derailed. His promises to Abraham, Isaac, and Jacob did not expire with the failures of their descendants.

Understanding what happened to the tribes in the centuries after their settlement is essential for understanding the Middle East conflict today. The divisions, the hatreds, the broken alliances, and the competing claims to the land that dominate our headlines did not emerge from a vacuum. They grew out of real historical fractures, and many of those fractures trace directly back to the period we are about to examine.

This chapter covers a vast sweep of history, from the rise of the Samaritans to the fall of Jerusalem, from the first king of Israel to the last king of Judah. It is a story that spans roughly five centuries, and every part of it has left its mark on the land and the peoples who continue to fight over it. If we are to understand the Middle East as God sees it, we must first understand how His people went from a United Kingdom under David and Solomon to a scattered remnant weeping by the rivers of Babylon.

The Rise of the Samaritans: A People Between Two Worlds

If you have spent any time reading the Gospels, you know that the Samaritans occupied a unique and largely unwelcome place in the world of first-century Judaism. When Jesus told the parable of the Good Samaritan in Luke 10, He was not simply choosing a random ethnic group to make a point about neighborly love. He was deliberately selecting the one people group that His Jewish audience would have found most offensive as the hero of the story. To understand why, we need to go back several centuries before Jesus and trace how the Samaritans came to exist in the first place.

The Samaritans occupied the territory that had once belonged to the tribe of Ephraim and the half-tribe of Manasseh, with their capital in the city of Samaria. This had been the heartland of the northern kingdom of Israel. When the Assyrian Empire conquered the northern kingdom in 722 BC and carried the ten tribes into captivity, they did not leave the land empty. The king of

Assyria imported people from several foreign nations, including Cutha, Ava, Hamath, and Sepharvaim, and resettled them in the territory of Samaria (2 Kings 17:24; Ezra 4:2-11). These foreign settlers intermarried with the Israelite population that remained in and around the region, and their descendants became the people known as the Samaritans.

What made the Samaritans particularly problematic in Jewish eyes was not simply the intermarriage. It was what happened to their worship. When these foreign settlers first arrived, they continued to worship the gods of their home nations. But when a plague of lions troubled the region, they concluded that they had failed to honor the god of the territory. A Jewish priest was sent from Assyria to instruct them in the religion of Jehovah, and they were taught from the books of Moses. However, they never fully abandoned their idolatrous practices. The result was a hybrid religion, a blend of Mosaic teaching and pagan custom, that was neither fully Jewish nor fully pagan (2 Kings 17:26-28). For the Jews, this was not a compromise. It was an abomination.

The animosity only deepened over time, and there were specific historical events that pushed the relationship between Jews and Samaritans past the point of recovery. First, when the Jews returned from Babylonian exile and began rebuilding the temple in Jerusalem, the Samaritans actively opposed the effort. During Nehemiah's rebuilding of the walls of Jerusalem, Samaritan leaders mounted a vigorous campaign to halt the construction (Nehemiah 6:1-14). For the returning Jewish exiles who had wept by the rivers of Babylon and longed for the restoration of their homeland, this Samaritan opposition was not merely a political inconvenience. It was an act of spiritual warfare. The Samaritans used every tool available to them: political lobbying with the Persian court, physical intimidation of the builders, and psychological warfare through threats and false rumors. Nehemiah records that the builders worked with a tool in one hand and a weapon in the other (Nehemiah 4:17), so real was the threat from their Samaritan neighbors.

Second, the Samaritans eventually built their own rival temple on Mount Gerizim. They insisted that this was the location Moses had designated for the nation's worship, and they established their own priesthood under a high priest named Manasses, the son-in-law of the Samaritan leader Sanballat. This competing worship center made the breach between Jews and Samaritans theological, not just ethnic. It was no longer simply a matter of who your parents were. It was a matter of where you worshiped and which priesthood you recognized. The Samaritans had created, in effect, a rival religion, one that claimed the authority of Moses while rejecting the authority of everything that came after him.

Third, Samaria became a refuge for Jewish outlaws and religious fugitives (Joshua 20:6-7; 21:21). Those who had been excommunicated from Jewish society or who were fleeing Jewish law could find safety among the Samaritans, who were happy to receive them. This only intensified the Jewish conviction that Samaria was a lawless place, a haven for those who had rejected the covenant community.

Fourth, and perhaps most significantly for the religious divide, the Samaritans accepted only the five books of Moses as Scripture. They rejected the prophets, the psalms, and all the traditions of rabbinic Judaism. For a devout Jew, this was not simply a matter of a shorter Bible. It was a rejection of the full revelation of God. The prophetic writings contained the messianic promises, the calls to repentance, the visions of Israel's future restoration, and the moral teachings that shaped every dimension of Jewish life. To reject the prophets was, in Jewish eyes, to reject the God who had spoken through them.

From these accumulated grievances arose what the Bible describes as an irreconcilable difference. The Jews regarded the Samaritans as the lowest of the low. In John 8:48, calling someone a Samaritan was used as an insult against Jesus Himself. John 4:9 tells us plainly that *"the Jews had no dealings with the Samaritans."* The hatred was not one-sided. The Samaritans harbored their own deep resentments toward the Jews, viewing them as arrogant, exclusionary, and wrong about the proper location of worship. It was a mutual hostility fed by centuries of grievance.

Yet it was precisely into this atmosphere of hostility that Jesus chose to enter. In one of the most remarkable conversations recorded in Scripture, Jesus met a Samaritan woman at Jacob's well and offered her the living water of eternal life (John 4:6–26). He did not merely tolerate her presence—He intentionally sought her out. The text tells us that Jesus *"had to go through Samaria"* (John 4:4). This statement speaks less about geography, since many Jews intentionally avoided Samaritan territory by taking a longer route, and more about divine purpose. Jesus went to Samaria because there was a woman there whom the Father intended to reach.

The conversation itself was radical on multiple levels. A Jewish rabbi speaking publicly with a woman was unusual enough. A Jewish rabbi speaking with a Samaritan woman was scandalous. A Jewish rabbi offering living water to a Samaritan woman with a troubled personal history was the kind of grace that shattered every social convention of the ancient world. When the disciples returned and found Jesus talking with her, the text says they *"were surprised"* (John 4:27), which is probably an understatement.

Later, the apostles would follow Jesus' example and preach the Gospel openly in Samaria (Acts 8:25). Philip the evangelist went down to a city in Samaria and proclaimed the Messiah there, and the response was overwhelming (Acts 8:5-8). Peter and John were later sent from Jerusalem to confirm what had happened, and when they laid hands on the Samaritan believers, the Holy Spirit fell upon them. The wall that had stood for centuries between Jew and Samaritan was not destroyed by political negotiation or military force. It was broken by grace. This is an important principle that we will return to when we examine the modern conflict in the Middle

East. Human divisions, no matter how ancient or deeply rooted, are never beyond the reach of the Gospel. What politics cannot resolve, Christ can reconcile.

The Samaritan story also carries a warning for the church in every generation. The Samaritans did not set out to create a false religion. They attempted to blend the worship of the true God with the cultural practices they had inherited. They kept portions of Scripture while discarding the rest. They maintained certain forms of devotion while mixing them with elements God had never sanctioned. The result was not merely a weaker version of true faith. It was something the Jews considered more offensive than outright paganism, because it wore the clothing of truth while promoting error. Whenever the church is tempted to accommodate the culture by diluting the full counsel of God, the Samaritan story stands as a reminder of where that road leads.

A Kingdom United: The First Three Kings

Before we can understand how the twelve tribes were scattered, we need to understand the brief and troubled period when they were united under a single monarchy. In the period of the Judges, Israel had no king, and the Book of Judges records the painful result: *"Everyone did as he saw fit"* (Judges 21:25). It was a season of moral chaos, tribal infighting, and spiritual decline. The final chapters of the Book of Judges describe events so horrifying, including a civil war that nearly exterminated the tribe of Benjamin, that the reader is left in no doubt about the desperate condition of the nation.

God raised up the prophet Samuel to lead the nation (1 Samuel 3:4). All Israel recognized that Samuel had been established as a prophet of the Lord (1 Samuel 3:20), and he judged the nation faithfully throughout his life. Samuel was a bridge figure, the last of the judges and the first of the great prophets who would stand alongside, and often against, the kings of Israel. But when

Samuel grew old and appointed his sons as judges over Israel, the people rejected them. His sons, Joel and Abijah, *"did not follow his ways. They turned aside after dishonest gain and accepted bribes and perverted justice"* (1 Samuel 8:3). The failure of Samuel's sons was not merely a family disappointment. It was a national crisis that would change the entire structure of Israelite society.

More than rejecting the sons, the people rejected the entire system of prophetic leadership and demanded a king, wanting to be *"like all the nations"* around them (1 Samuel 8:19-20). When Samuel brought their request to God, the Lord's response was both gracious and sobering: "Listen to them and give them a king" (1 Samuel 8:22). But God also instructed Samuel to warn the people what a king would cost them: their sons would be taken for his army, their daughters for his kitchens and perfumeries, their best fields and vineyards would be seized, and a tenth of their flocks would be demanded as royal tax (1 Samuel 8:11-18). The people heard the warning and dismissed it. *"No!" they said. "We want a king over us"* (1 Samuel 8:19).

There is a lesson here that echoes throughout Scripture and resonates in our own time. God sometimes allows us to have what we ask for, even when what we ask for is not what is best for us. Israel wanted a king, and God gave them one. But the road ahead would prove that the human desire for visible, earthly authority often leads to disappointment.

Saul: The King Who Lost His Way

Saul, Israel's first king, came from the tribe of Benjamin, a tribe that had nearly been wiped out during the period of the judges. He was tall, handsome, and humble at the start. When Samuel first identified him as God's chosen king, Saul protested: *"Am I not a Benjamite, from the smallest tribe of Israel, and is not my clan the least of all the clans of the tribe of Benjamin? Why do you say such a thing to me?"* (1 Samuel 9:21). This initial humility was genuine and attractive. On the day of his public presentation as king, Saul was so reluctant that he hid among the baggage (1 Samuel 10:22).

His reign began with a brilliant military victory over the Ammonites at Jabesh-gilead, and whatever doubts the people had about the monarchy initially disappeared. There was a moment of genuine national unity and hope. But success went to Saul's head with remarkable speed. Humility gave way to pride. He offered a sacrifice at Gilgal that was the exclusive function of priests, refusing to wait for Samuel as he had been instructed. This was not a minor procedural error. It revealed a presumption about his own authority that would define his reign. Samuel's rebuke was devastating: *"You have done a foolish thing. You have not kept the command the Lord your God gave you"* (1 Samuel 13:13).

The second major act of disobedience sealed Saul's fate. God commanded him to completely destroy the Amalekites, including their livestock. Saul defeated the Amalekites but spared their king, Agag, and kept the best of the sheep and cattle, claiming he intended to sacrifice them to God. Samuel's response contains one of the most quoted principles in all of Scripture: *"Does the Lord delight in burnt offerings and sacrifices as much as in obeying the Lord? To obey is better than sacrifice, and to heed is better than the fat of rams"* (1 Samuel 15:22). God told Samuel, *"I am grieved that I have made Saul king, because he has turned away from me and has not carried out my instructions"* (1 Samuel 15:10).

From that point on, Saul's reign was a slow descent into darkness. The Spirit of the Lord departed from him, and a *"harmful spirit"* tormented him (1 Samuel 16:14). He became consumed with jealousy toward the young David, whose military successes made him popular with the people. Saul spent years pursuing David through the wilderness, trying to kill him, while neglecting his duties as king. He consulted a medium at Endor in direct violation of God's law.

In the end, wounded in battle against the Philistines on Mount Gilboa, he *"took his own sword and fell on it"* (1 Samuel 31:4). His sons, including Jonathan, David's beloved friend, died alongside him. Saul reigned from approximately 1049 to 1009 BC. It was a tragic conclusion to a reign that had begun with so much promise. Saul's story is a warning to every leader: giftedness without obedience is not enough. Outward stature without inward submission to God leads inevitably to ruin.

David: The Man After God's Heart

David had been anointed king as a boy by Samuel, but he did not ascend to the throne until after Saul's death (2 Samuel 2:4). He was short of stature, ruddy, of beautiful countenance, and possessed immense physical strength and personal attractiveness. More importantly, he was described as a man after God's own heart (1 Samuel 13:14; Acts 13:22). He was a warrior, a musician, a poet, and a man of deep, if imperfect, faith.

David's early years read like an adventure story. He killed the giant Goliath with a sling and a stone when he was still a shepherd boy (1 Samuel 17). He served in Saul's court, married Saul's daughter Michal, and formed one of the deepest friendships in all of Scripture with Saul's son Jonathan. When Saul turned against him, David spent years living as a fugitive in the wilderness of Judea, leading a band of outcasts and misfits who would later become his most loyal military commanders. Throughout those years of persecution, David consistently refused to harm Saul, recognizing that Saul was still the Lord's anointed. On two separate occasions when David had the opportunity to kill Saul, he refused (1 Samuel 24; 26). This restraint reveals the quality that set David apart: a reverence for God's authority that transcended personal ambition.

God made David a promise that would echo through the rest of biblical history: his family line would reign forever. The prophet Isaiah gave this promise its most vivid expression: *"A shoot will come up from the stump of Jesse [David's father] and from his roots a Branch will bear fruit"* (Isaiah 11:1). That Branch, Christians understand, is Jesus Christ, the Son of David, whose kingdom will have no end.

After Saul's death, David was first made king over the tribe of Judah at Hebron, and seven years later he was made king over all Israel. He was thirty years old when he began to reign and ruled from approximately 1009 to 969 BC. David conquered Jerusalem from the Jebusites and made it his capital, establishing it as the political and spiritual center of the nation. He brought the Ark of the Covenant to Jerusalem with great celebration, dancing before the Lord *"with all his might"* (2 Samuel 6:14). He desired to build a permanent temple for the Ark, but God told him that this task would fall to his son instead. However, God promised David something far greater than a building: an eternal dynasty.

> *"When your days are over and you rest with your ancestors, I will raise up your offspring to succeed you, your own flesh and blood, and I will establish his kingdom. He is the one who will build a house for my Name, and I will establish the throne of his kingdom forever." (2 Samuel 7:12-13)*

David's failures are as well-documented as his triumphs. His adultery with Bathsheba, his murder of her husband Uriah, the devastating family consequences that followed, including the rebellion of his own son Absalom, are recorded with unflinching honesty. Scripture does not hide David's sins. But neither does it reduce him to his worst moments. When confronted by the prophet Nathan, David's response was immediate and genuine: *"I have sinned against the Lord"* (2 Samuel 12:13). Psalm 51, his great prayer of repentance, has been the model for penitent believers ever since.

For all his failures, and Scripture does not hide them, David remains the standard against which every subsequent king of Israel and Judah would be measured. The phrase *"he did what was right in the eyes of the Lord, as his father David had done"* or its negative counterpart appears again and again in the books of Kings and Chronicles. David's life teaches us that God does not require perfection. He requires a heart that, when it falls, falls toward Him.

Solomon: Wisdom, Glory, and the Seeds of Division

Solomon became king around 971 BC, possibly serving as co-regent with his aging father David for a short period, and reigned until approximately 931 BC. He was the son of Bathsheba, and although he was not the natural heir by birth order, he was chosen by David and approved by God to succeed him on the throne (1 Chronicles 23:1). His accession was not without controversy. His older brother Adonijah attempted to seize the throne, but the combined intervention of Nathan the prophet, Bathsheba, and David himself ensured that Solomon was anointed as king.

Solomon inherited what was arguably the most powerful kingdom on earth at that time. It was an era of peace, prosperity, vast commercial enterprise, and literary achievement. Solomon's wisdom became legendary. Kings and queens from distant nations traveled to hear him speak. The Queen of Sheba, after visiting his court, declared: *"The report I heard in my own country about your achievements and your wisdom is true. But I did not believe these things until I came and saw with my own eyes. Indeed, not even half was told me; in wisdom and wealth you have far exceeded the report I heard"* (1 Kings 10:6-7).

When God told Solomon to ask for whatever he wanted, Solomon asked for wisdom to govern his people. This request pleased God, who richly rewarded him with not only wisdom but also wealth, power, and the extraordinary privilege of building the temple in Jerusalem (1 Chronicles 28:2-6). The construction of the temple was the crowning achievement of Solomon's reign and one of the defining events in Israel's history. It took seven years to build and was constructed with the finest materials available: cedar from Lebanon, gold, bronze, and precious stones. When the temple was completed and the Ark of the Covenant was placed in the Most Holy Place, the glory of the Lord filled the building so intensely that the priests could not stand to minister (1 Kings 8:10-11). But Solomon's reign also contained the seeds of catastrophe. His later years were marked by the accumulation of foreign wives who turned his heart toward the worship of their gods. The wisest man in the world made the most foolish of choices, and the consequences would outlast him by centuries.

First Kings 11 records the painful details. Solomon loved many foreign women, including Moabites, Ammonites, Edomites, Sidonians, and Hittites, all from nations about which God had specifically warned Israel not to intermarry. He had seven hundred wives of royal birth and three hundred concubines. These women turned his heart after other gods, and Solomon went after Ashtoreth, the goddess of the Sidonians, and after Milcom, the detestable god of the Ammonites. He even built high places for Chemosh and for Molech on the hill east of Jerusalem. The man who had built the temple of Jehovah now built shrines to pagan deities within sight of it.

God's response was direct: because Solomon had done this and had not kept the covenant, God would tear the kingdom away from his son, leaving only one tribe for the sake of David and for the sake of Jerusalem. Even in judgment, we see God's mercy. He did not tear the kingdom away during Solomon's lifetime, for David's sake. And He preserved one tribe, Judah, for the sake of the Davidic covenant and the messianic promise that depended on it.

There is a sobering application here for anyone who studies the Middle East conflict. The division of God's people, the fracturing of the covenant community, the weakening of the nation that was supposed to be a light to the world, did not begin with an external enemy. It began with internal compromise. The seeds of Israel's later vulnerability to Assyria, Babylon, Persia, Greece, and Rome were planted not by foreign armies but by a king who allowed his affections to be divided. When we look at the fractured state of the Promised Land today, we would do well to remember that the cracks in the foundation go all the way back to Solomon's bedroom.

A Kingdom Torn in Two

After Solomon's death in approximately 931 BC, the kingdom shattered. Ten tribes broke away to form the Northern Kingdom, which retained the name Israel. The tribes of Judah and Benjamin remained together as the Southern Kingdom, called Judah. This division was not merely a political event. It was a covenant crisis, a tearing of the fabric that God had woven when He brought Israel out of Egypt and established them as one nation under His law.

The immediate cause was the arrogance of Solomon's son Rehoboam. When the people came to him at Shechem asking for relief from the heavy taxation and forced labor his father had imposed, Rehoboam consulted two groups of advisors. The elders who had served Solomon counseled moderation: *"If today you will be a servant to these people and serve them and give them a favorable answer, they will always be your servants"* (1 Kings 12:7). The young men who had grown up with Rehoboam counseled severity: tell the people your father was hard, but you will be harder still.

Rehoboam followed the advice of the young men. His answer to the people's plea was breathtaking in its arrogance: *"My father made your yoke heavy; I will make it even heavier. My father scourged you with whips; I will scourge you with scorpions"* (1 Kings 12:14). The ten northern tribes immediately revolted. "What share do we have in David?" they cried. *"To your tents, Israel!"* (1 Kings 12:16). The kingdom that David had fought to unite and Solomon had adorned with splendor was torn in two in a single day.

But the deeper cause was the spiritual rot that had been spreading through the nation for decades, a drift away from wholehearted devotion to God that left the kingdom vulnerable to fracture. Solomon's idolatry had weakened the spiritual bonds that held the tribes together. When the political crisis came, there was no reservoir of covenant loyalty deep enough to hold the nation together. What followed was a long, painful history of two parallel kingdoms, each with its own line of rulers, its own trajectory of faithfulness and apostasy, and its own eventual encounter with divine judgment. The date of the division, approximately 931 BC, is one of the most important dates in the biblical timeline. Everything that follows, including the scattering of the tribes, the Assyrian and Babylonian exiles, the rise of the Samaritans, and the conditions that shaped the world into which Jesus was born, flows from this catastrophic split.

The Kings of Israel: A Catalog of Unfaithfulness

The Northern Kingdom of Israel lasted from approximately 931 to 722 BC, a span of roughly two centuries. In that entire time, not a single one of its twenty kings was faithful to Jehovah. Every king practiced idolatry, and the worst among them promoted the worship of Baal, the Canaanite fertility god whose rituals included temple prostitution and practices that Scripture describes as detestable.

Jeroboam I, the first king of the Northern Kingdom (931 to 910 BC), set the pattern by establishing golden calves at Bethel and Dan to prevent his people from traveling to Jerusalem to worship. His reasoning was political: if the people continued to go to the temple in Jerusalem, their loyalty might return to the house of David. So he created a rival worship system, complete with its own feast days and its own priesthood drawn from outside the tribe of Levi. His rebellious innovation became the benchmark of evil: later biblical writers would repeatedly condemn subsequent kings for walking *"in the way of Jeroboam."* From that poisoned beginning, the northern monarchy descended through twenty kings, most of whose reigns were marked by assassination, conspiracy, and spiritual corruption.

Ahab (874 to 853 BC) stands out as perhaps the worst of the lot. He married the Phoenician princess Jezebel, a woman whose name has become synonymous with religious seduction and spiritual compromise throughout the history of the church. Jezebel was not content merely to worship her own gods in private. She launched a systematic campaign to establish Baal worship as the state religion of Israel and to exterminate the prophets of Jehovah. She supported 450 prophets of Baal and 400 prophets of Asherah at the royal table (1 Kings 18:19).

It was during Ahab's reign that the prophet Elijah stood alone on Mount Carmel and challenged the prophets of Baal in one of the most dramatic confrontations in all of Scripture (1 Kings 18). Elijah proposed a test: both he and the prophets of Baal would prepare a sacrifice, and the god who answered by fire would be acknowledged as the true God. The prophets of Baal called on their god from morning until evening, cutting themselves with knives and dancing around the altar. Nothing happened. Elijah, after mocking their silence, *"Call louder! Perhaps he is deep in thought, or busy, or traveling"* (1 Kings 18:27), drenched his own sacrifice with water, prayed a simple prayer, and fire fell from heaven and consumed everything, the sacrifice, the wood, the stones, the water, and the dust. The people fell on their faces and cried, *"The Lord, He is God! The Lord, He is God!"* (1 Kings 18:39).

Jehu (841 to 814 BC) earns the distinction of being *"not good but better than the rest,"* which gives you a sense of how low the bar had fallen. Jehu destroyed Baal worship in Israel by massacring the worshipers of Baal in the temple itself (2 Kings 10:18-28). But he did not turn away from the golden calves that Jeroboam had set up, and God's assessment was mixed: partial obedience credited but full faithfulness lacking.

The political instability of the Northern Kingdom was staggering. Several of its kings came to power through assassination. Nadab was murdered by Baasha, who then killed every member of Jeroboam's family. Elah was assassinated by Zimri while drunk at a party. Zimri reigned for only seven days before setting fire to the royal palace with himself inside when he saw his cause was lost. Shallum killed Zechariah and reigned for just one month before being killed by Menahem, who then attacked the city of Tiphsah and *"ripped open all the pregnant women"* (2 Kings 15:16) in an act of terror that reveals the moral depths to which the kingdom had sunk. Pekahiah was assassinated by Pekah, who was in turn overthrown by Hoshea, the final king, during whose reign Assyria completed its conquest.

The Northern Kingdom did not simply decline. It convulsed, lurching from one violent transition to the next, each new king inheriting the spiritual poison that Jeroboam had introduced at the very beginning. Throughout this long descent, God did not leave the Northern Kingdom without a witness. The prophets Elijah and Elisha ministered during the reigns of some of the worst kings, performing miracles, confronting idolatry, and calling the nation to repentance. Elisha's ministry alone included the healing of Naaman the Syrian, the multiplication of the widow's oil, the raising of the Shunammite woman's son, and the feeding of a hundred men with twenty loaves of bread, a miracle that foreshadowed Jesus' feeding of the five thousand. Later, Amos and Hosea spoke God's words to a people who were rushing headlong toward judgment.

Hosea's ministry is particularly poignant. God commanded him to marry an unfaithful woman named Gomer, and their troubled marriage became a living parable of God's relationship with Israel: a faithful husband pursuing a wife who had given herself to other lovers. Hosea's pain was God's pain. His heartbreak was a reflection of the divine heartbreak over a nation that had been loved, provided for, and blessed beyond measure, yet had turned to worship gods of wood and stone. The prophets made it clear that the coming judgment was not arbitrary. It was the direct consequence of choices the nation had made.

The Northern Kingdom ended in 722 BC when the Assyrian Empire under Shalmaneser V, and then his successor Sargon II, conquered Samaria and carried the population into exile. The

Assyrian practice of deportation was designed to break the national identity of conquered peoples. Populations were relocated hundreds of miles from their homeland, scattered among other displaced groups, and stripped of the cultural and religious ties that held them together as a people. The ten tribes were scattered across the vast Assyrian territory, and it was into their former homeland that the foreign settlers who would become the Samaritans were imported.

The northern tribes effectively disappeared from the historical stage as distinct, identifiable groups, giving rise to centuries of speculation about the so-called "lost tribes of Israel." Various theories have placed these lost tribes everywhere from Ethiopia to Japan to the British Isles, but the biblical evidence suggests a simpler reality: the northern tribes were absorbed into the populations among whom they were scattered, losing their distinct tribal identity through intermarriage and cultural assimilation. This was precisely what the Assyrians intended.

The term "Lost Tribes of Israel" refers to the ten northern tribes that were taken into exile following the Assyrian conquest of the Northern Kingdom of Israel in 722 B.C. After the death of King Solomon, the United Kingdom of Israel divided into two parts: the northern kingdom called Israel (composed of ten tribes) and the southern kingdom called Judah (primarily Judah and Benjamin). Because of persistent idolatry and covenant unfaithfulness, God allowed the Assyrian Empire to conquer the northern kingdom and deport many of its inhabitants to distant regions of the empire (2 Kings 17:6). Over time these tribes were dispersed among other nations, and their distinct tribal identities gradually disappeared from historical record, leading to their designation as the "lost tribes."

Although they are often called "lost," Scripture indicates that God's covenant purposes for Israel were not abandoned. The prophets frequently spoke of a future restoration in which God would gather His scattered people from among the nations (Ezekiel 37:21–22; Isaiah 11:11–12). In the New Testament, references such as James 1:1, addressed *"to the twelve tribes scattered abroad,"* suggest that the concept of Israel's dispersed tribes remained theologically significant. Ultimately, the theme of the lost tribes points to God's ongoing redemptive plan for His people and His faithfulness to His covenant promises, demonstrating that even dispersion and judgment do not nullify God's sovereign purposes in salvation history.

The lesson of the Northern Kingdom is a sobering one. A nation or a people can be given extraordinary blessings, a promised land, a covenant relationship with God, a heritage of miraculous deliverance, and still lose everything through persistent unfaithfulness. The Northern Kingdom did not fall because God's promises failed. It fell because the people abandoned the God who had made those promises.

The Kings of Judah: A More Complex Story

The Southern Kingdom of Judah had a longer and more complex history, lasting from approximately 931 to 586 BC, when Jerusalem fell to the Babylonians. Unlike the Northern Kingdom, Judah's story includes genuine spiritual revivals alongside terrible periods of apostasy. Some of its kings were faithful; others were among the worst leaders in Israel's history. The Davidic dynasty provided continuity that the north never had, and the presence of the temple in Jerusalem gave Judah a spiritual anchor that persisted even through its darkest periods.

Asa (911 to 870 BC) and Jehoshaphat (873 to 848 BC) were righteous kings who led genuine reforms and sought the Lord with sincerity. Asa removed the foreign altars and high places, smashed the sacred stones and cut down the Asherah poles. He even deposed his own grandmother, Maakah, from her position as queen mother because she had made a repulsive image for Asherah (1 Kings 15:13). This took real courage. Jehoshaphat continued and deepened his father's reforms, sending Levites throughout the cities of Judah to teach the people from the

Book of the Law (2 Chronicles 17:7-9). During Jehoshaphat's reign, the surrounding nations were so impressed by Judah's military and spiritual strength that they brought tribute rather than war.

Hezekiah (715 to 686 BC) stands out as the best of Judah's kings, a man who *"trusted in the Lord, the God of Israel. There was no one like him among all the kings of Judah, either before him or after him"* (2 Kings 18:5). He reopened and purified the temple that his father Ahaz had closed and defiled. He organized the greatest Passover celebration since the days of Solomon, inviting not only Judah but also the remnant of the northern tribes to come to Jerusalem and worship. When the Assyrian army under Sennacherib besieged Jerusalem and sent a messenger to mock the God of Israel, Hezekiah went to the temple, spread the threatening letter before the Lord, and prayed. God answered by sending an angel who struck down 185,000 Assyrian soldiers in a single night (2 Kings 19:35). It was one of the most dramatic divine interventions in the entire Old Testament.

Josiah (640 to 609 BC) was another great reformer. He came to the throne at the age of eight, after the assassination of his wicked father Amon. When he was twenty-six, during renovations of the temple, the high priest Hilkiah discovered a copy of the Book of the Law that had been lost or hidden during the decades of apostasy under Manasseh and Amon. When the book was read to Josiah, he tore his robes in grief and launched the most thoroughgoing religious reform Judah had ever seen. He destroyed the high places, smashed the idols, and reinstituted the Passover. The text says of him: *"Neither before nor after Josiah was there a king like him who turned to the Lord as he did, with all his heart and with all his soul and with all his strength"* (2 Kings 23:25). The discovery of Scripture, and the national repentance it provoked, is one of the most encouraging episodes in the entire biblical narrative.

But Judah also produced kings like Ahaz (735 to 715 BC), who practiced child sacrifice and shut the doors of the temple, and Manasseh (695 to 642 BC), who was so depraved that the biblical writers attribute the eventual fall of Jerusalem directly to his sins. Manasseh reigned for fifty-five years, the longest reign of any king of Judah, and he filled every one of those years with abomination. He rebuilt the high places his father Hezekiah had destroyed, erected altars to Baal, worshiped the stars of heaven, practiced sorcery and divination, and, most horrifically, sacrificed his own son in the fire (2 Kings 21:1-9). He *"shed so much innocent blood that he filled Jerusalem from end to end"* (2 Kings 21:16).

However, Judah also produced kings such as Ahaz (735–715 B.C.), who practiced child sacrifice and even shut the doors of the temple, leading the nation deeper into idolatry. Later came Manasseh (695–642 B.C.), whose reign became one of the darkest periods in Judah's history. The biblical writers connect the eventual fall of Jerusalem directly to the depth of his wickedness. Manasseh ruled for fifty-five years—the longest reign of any king of Judah and much of that time was marked by spiritual corruption and moral decline.

During his reign, Manasseh reversed the reforms of his father Hezekiah by rebuilding the high places that had been destroyed. He erected altars to Baal, worshiped the host of heaven, practiced sorcery and divination, and committed the horrific act of sacrificing his own son in the fire (2 Kings 21:1–9). His rule was characterized not only by idolatry but also by extreme violence, as Scripture records that he "shed so much innocent blood that he filled Jerusalem from one end to another" (2 Kings 21:16). His leadership plunged the nation into profound spiritual darkness and contributed significantly to the judgment that would later come upon Judah.

Manasseh's story, however, includes a remarkable epilogue. At the very end of his life, the Assyrians took him captive, bound him with bronze shackles, and carried him to Babylon. In his distress, Manasseh *"sought the favor of the Lord his God and humbled himself greatly before the God of his ancestors. And when he prayed to him, the Lord was moved by his entreaty and listened to his plea"* (2 Chronicles 33:12-13). Manasseh was restored to his throne and spent his final years attempting to undo the damage he had caused. It is a reminder that even the most wicked life can find mercy in genuine repentance. But the damage of fifty-five years of depravity could not be reversed in a few years of reform. The nation had been corrupted too deeply.

The contrast between the best and worst kings of Judah illustrates a principle that runs throughout Scripture: the character of leadership determines the trajectory of a nation. When Hezekiah led, Judah was miraculously delivered. When Josiah led, the nation was reformed. When Manasseh and Ahaz led, the nation was destroyed from within. Individual leadership decisions have consequences that ripple across generations.

The final kings of Judah presided over a rapid decline. Jehoahaz reigned only three months before being deposed by Pharaoh Necho of Egypt. Jehoiakim (609 to 597 BC) was a puppet king installed by Egypt who later became a vassal of Babylon. In one of the most defiant acts recorded in Scripture, he took the scroll on which Jeremiah's prophecies had been written, and as each section was read aloud, he cut it off with a scribe's knife and threw it into the fire, *"until the entire scroll was burned in the fire"* (Jeremiah 36:23). He showed no fear and no remorse. Jehoiachin reigned for only three months before being carried to Babylon by Nebuchadnezzar. Zedekiah (597 to 586 BC), the last king, ignored Jeremiah's counsel to submit to Babylon, rebelled, and watched as his city was besieged, his sons were killed before his eyes, and then his own eyes were put out before he was carried in chains to Babylon.

The Babylonian exile of 586 BC was the defining catastrophe of Israel's history before the coming of Christ. It marked the end of the monarchy, the destruction of the temple that Solomon had built, and the scattering of God's people into a foreign land. The book of Lamentations, traditionally attributed to Jeremiah, captures the anguish of the survivors in language of devastating beauty.

"How deserted lies the city, once so full of people! How like a widow is she, who once was great among the nations! She who was queen among the provinces has now become a slave." (Lamentations 1:1)

And yet, even in that darkest hour, the prophets held out hope. Jeremiah promised a return from exile: *"When seventy years are completed for Babylon, I will come to you and fulfill my good promise to bring you back to this place"* (Jeremiah 29:10). Ezekiel saw a vision of a valley of dry bones coming to life under the breath of God (Ezekiel 37), a prophecy of national resurrection that has stirred the hearts of Jewish people for twenty-six centuries. Isaiah spoke of a Suffering Servant who would bear the sins of His people (Isaiah 53), a prophecy that Christians understand as pointing directly to Jesus Christ. The scattering of the tribes was not the end of the story. It was, in God's sovereign plan, a preparation for the next great chapter.

Why This History Matters Today

The story of the kings and the divided monarchy may seem far removed from the modern headlines about Israel and Palestine, about Hamas and the Israel Defense Forces; IDF, about territorial disputes and ceasefire negotiations. But these ancient events established patterns that continue to shape the region and the conflict to this day. The Israel Defense Forces were established in 1948 following the creation of the State of Israel. The IDF unified several pre-state Jewish paramilitary organizations, including the Haganah, Irgun, and Lehi, into one national military structure.

Consider the pattern of division. The kingdom split because a leader chose pride over wisdom, because the people's grievances were dismissed rather than addressed, and because generations of accumulated spiritual compromise had weakened the bonds that held the nation together. Is this pattern not familiar? The modern Middle East is defined by divisions that began with specific choices, specific grievances, and specific failures of leadership. Understanding the ancient pattern does not give us a political solution, but it does give us a theological lens for seeing the conflict more clearly.

The Northern Kingdom's disappearance created the Samaritan problem, which in turn contributed to the fractured identity of the land. The Babylonian exile reshaped Jewish identity around the synagogue and the Torah, creating the Judaism that Jesus encountered and that continues to this day. The promises made to David established the messianic hope that remains central to both Jewish and Christian theology. And the repeated cycle of faithfulness, apostasy, judgment, and restoration reveals a pattern of God's dealings with His people that is as relevant in the twenty-first century as it was in the ninth century BC.

Consider also the role of exile. The Babylonian exile did not destroy the Jewish people. It refined them. The loss of the temple, the monarchy, and the land forced the Jews to rediscover the core of their identity in the Word of God itself. The synagogue system, the preservation of Scripture, the development of rabbinic teaching, all of these emerged from the crucible of exile. When the Jewish people returned to the land under Ezra and Nehemiah, they were a different people, more conscious of their covenant identity, more devoted to the study of Torah, more determined never again to fall into the idolatry that had caused their downfall. The exile that seemed like the end was actually a painful but necessary preparation for the next stage of God's plan.

Consider, finally, the role of the prophets. Throughout the darkest periods of Israel's history, God always maintained a prophetic witness. Elijah stood alone on Mount Carmel. Jeremiah preached to a city that mocked him and threw him in a cistern. Hosea married a woman who broke his heart so that his life could be a sermon about God's love. These men spoke truth to power at great personal cost, and the record of their faithfulness has been preserved for us in

Scripture. In every generation, God raises up voices that speak His word into the chaos of human events. The question is never whether God is speaking. The question is whether anyone is listening.

Most importantly, the scattering of the tribes fulfilled specific prophetic warnings while simultaneously setting the stage for prophetic promises that remain unfulfilled. The God who scattered also promised to regather. The God who judged also promised to restore. And those promises of regathering and restoration are at the very heart of what we see unfolding in the Middle East today. In the next chapter, we will turn our attention to one of the most significant theological developments in the biblical narrative: the separation of humanity into Jews and Gentiles, and what that division means for God's plan of redemption.

Chapter 9

THE GREAT DIVIDE: JEWS AND GENTILES

"For he is our peace, who hath made both one, and hath broken down the middle wall of partition between us." (Ephesians 2:14, KJV)

If you have grown up in the church, you have probably heard the words Jew and Gentile so many times that they have become almost invisible, like wallpaper in a room you walk through every day. We use these terms in sermons, Bible studies, and theological discussions without always stopping to consider what they really mean, where they came from, or why the distinction matters. But if we are going to understand the Middle East conflict through the lens of Scripture, we cannot afford to treat these categories casually. The division of humanity into Jews and Gentiles is not a footnote in God's plan. It is one of the central organizing realities of biblical history, and its implications reach all the way from Genesis to Revelation.

In this chapter, we will trace the origins of this great divide, examine the meaning of terms like Hebrew, Israelite, and Jew, and then turn to the New Testament to see how the apostle Paul addressed the relationship between Jews and Gentiles in light of the Gospel. What we discover will have direct bearing on how we understand the promises God made concerning the land, the people, and the future of the Middle East.

This is also a chapter that requires us to hold two truths in tension. On the one hand, the distinction between Jew and Gentile is real, divinely established, and permanently significant in God's prophetic plan. On the other hand, the Gospel of Jesus Christ has destroyed the hostility between the two groups and created a new humanity in which both are welcomed on equal terms into the family of God. Understanding how both of these things can be true at the same time is essential for any Christian who wants to think clearly about Israel, the Arab world, and the conflict that has defined their relationship for millennia.

When Did the Separation Begin?

There is no single verse in Scripture that announces, *"On this day, God separated the Jews from the Gentiles."* The division developed gradually, and Bible scholars have proposed two primary ways of understanding its origins. The first view holds that the separation effectively began with the descendants of Adam and Eve. According to this perspective, the chosen line of Seth was always distinct from the rest of humanity. Seth's descendants, who called upon the name of the Lord (Genesis 4:26), were considered the spiritual ancestors of the Jewish people, while the rest of humanity, descended through Cain and the other children of Adam, represented the Gentile nations. This view points to the fact that the Book of Genesis traces Seth's genealogy in painstaking detail all the way to Noah (Genesis 5), while giving only a brief summary of Cain's line. The focus of Scripture is relentlessly on this chosen line, and everything outside it, no matter how populous or powerful, is treated as background.

The second view, which carries stronger biblical support, places the formal separation at the calling of Abraham in Genesis 12. It was at that moment that God singled out one man and one family line for a specific covenantal purpose: to be the vehicle through which all the nations of the earth would be blessed. Before Abraham, there was certainly a chosen line of ancestry. The genealogies make that clear. But there was no formal national identity, no covenant community set apart from the surrounding peoples with specific laws, practices, and territorial promises.

There is truth in both perspectives. There was always a chosen line. From Seth through Noah, from Shem through Eber, from Terah through Abraham, the thread of God's redemptive purpose runs through specific individuals and their descendants. The genealogy of Seth is traced all the way to Noah (Genesis 5), then to Abraham (Genesis 11), then to the twelve sons of Jacob (Exodus 1), then through the kings of Judah (1 and 2 Kings), and ultimately to the birth of Jesus Christ Himself (Matthew 1; Luke 3). That unbroken line is one of the most remarkable features of the biblical narrative. It means that when you open the first page of Matthew's Gospel and read, *"The book of the genealogy of Jesus Christ, the son of David, the son of Abraham"* (Matthew 1:1), you are reading the final entry in a family register that stretches all the way back to the Garden of Eden.

However, the existence of a chosen line does not automatically mean there was always a formal separation of Jews and Gentiles as distinct categories of humanity. Until the time of Abraham, and then more fully defined in the time of Moses, the chosen line was not yet set apart as a nation with laws, rituals, and territorial boundaries that distinguished them from all other peoples. Noah was in the chosen line, but he was not a Jew. Shem was in the chosen line, but he was not an Israelite. The formal national identity that we associate with the terms Jew and Israelite did not exist until God created it through His covenant with Abraham and its elaboration through Moses.

It seems most biblically accurate to say that the formal division did not occur until God called Abraham. But even within Abraham's family, not every descendant belonged to the chosen line. Abraham's son Ishmael, as we have discussed in earlier chapters, was not the son of promise. Abraham's grandson Esau voluntarily sold his birthright and despised his covenantal inheritance.

A more precise placement of the division, then, would be with Jacob, whose name God changed to Israel (Genesis 32:28). All of Jacob's descendants, through his twelve sons, became the founding members of God's chosen nation. From that point forward, the line was clearly drawn.

God reiterated His promises concerning the land to Isaac (Genesis 26:3-5) and to Jacob (Genesis 28:13-15). In Genesis 35:12, God made this declaration to Jacob: *"The land I gave to Abraham and Isaac I also give to you, and I will give this land to your descendants after you."* The narrowing is unmistakable. Abraham had many sons. Isaac had two. But only Jacob, renamed Israel, and his twelve sons constitute the covenant nation. Everyone else, including Ishmael's twelve princes and Esau's tribal chiefs and Keturah's six sons and their vast descendants, falls outside the covenant line. They are, by definition, Gentiles.

What Was God's Purpose in This Separation?

This is a question that matters enormously, because it is easily misunderstood. The separation of Jews from Gentiles was never about superiority. It was about mission. God's desire for the Jewish people was that they would be a blessing to the entire world (Genesis 12:2-3). They were called to teach the nations about the one true God (Acts 13:46-47). Israel was to be a nation of priests, prophets, and missionaries, a kingdom of spiritual ambassadors whose lives and worship would point every surrounding nation toward the Creator and His promised Redeemer (Exodus 19:4-6).

> *"Now if you obey me fully and keep my covenant, then out of all nations you will be my treasured possession. Although the whole earth is mine, you will be for me a kingdom of priests and a holy nation." (Exodus 19:5-6)*

This passage is crucial for understanding God's intent. Israel was chosen not to hoard blessing but to distribute it. A priest does not exist for his own benefit. A priest stands between

God and the people, mediating God's truth to the world and the world's needs to God. Israel was supposed to be a priestly nation, a people whose entire national existence was oriented toward making God known to the surrounding peoples.

God's intent was for Israel to be a distinct people, visibly different in their worship, their ethics, and their national life, so that the contrast between life under God's covenant and life apart from it would be unmistakable (Deuteronomy 26:18-19). The dietary laws, the Sabbath observance, the sacrificial system, the festivals, the laws governing agriculture, commerce, justice, and family life, all of these were designed not merely as religious rules but as a visible testimony. When a neighboring nation observed that Israel rested every seventh day, that Israel's courts treated the poor with the same justice as the wealthy, that Israel's worship involved no images and no temple prostitution, these observations were meant to provoke a question: "Who is their God, and why does He produce a people like this?"

The Law given through Moses was not merely a legal code. It was a teaching tool, what Paul later called a *"guardian"* or *"schoolmaster"* that was designed to lead people to Christ (Galatians 3:23-24). Every lamb sacrificed on the altar pointed forward to the Lamb of God who would take away the sin of the world. Every Day of Atonement foreshadowed the day when the true High Priest would enter the heavenly Holy of Holies with His own blood. Every Passover meal recalled the night when God's judgment passed over the houses marked with the blood of the lamb, a picture of salvation through substitutionary sacrifice that finds its ultimate fulfillment in the cross of Jesus Christ.

The tragedy of Israel's history, as we saw in the previous chapter, is that the nation repeatedly failed in this mission. Rather than being a light to the nations, Israel often adopted the practices of the surrounding nations. Rather than drawing Gentiles toward Jehovah, Israel's kings led their own people toward Baal. But God's purpose was never nullified by human failure. The mission He assigned to Israel would ultimately be fulfilled, not through the nation's obedience, but through the coming of One who would perfectly embody Israel's calling: Jesus Christ, the light of the world.

Understanding the Terms: Hebrews, Israelites, and Jews

Before we go further, we need to untangle three terms that are often used interchangeably but actually carry distinct meanings. Understanding these distinctions will help us read both the Old and New Testaments with greater precision, and it will shed light on the identity claims that are central to the modern conflict in the Middle East.

Who Are the Hebrews?

The Hebrews are, broadly speaking, the people descended from Abraham. The origin of the word Hebrew is thought to come from the proper name *"Eber,"* listed in Genesis 10:24 as the great-grandson of Shem and an ancestor of Abraham. From Shem, through Arpachshad and Shelah, came Eber, the eponymous ancestor of the Hebrews. And Eber's descendant, through Peleg, Reu, Serug, and Nahor, was Terah, the father of Abraham and his brothers Nahor and Haran. Another possible etymology traces the root word back to a phrase meaning *"from the other side,"* which would make Hebrew a word designating an immigrant or a person who crossed over. This fits Abraham perfectly, since God called him to leave his homeland and cross into a land he had never seen (Genesis 12:1, 4-5). Abraham was, in the most literal sense, a man who came from the other side.

Abraham is the first person called a *"Hebrew"* in the Bible (Genesis 14:13). The context is significant: he is identified as "Abram the Hebrew" to distinguish him from the Canaanite, Amorite, and other tribal groups among whom he was living. The label marked him as an outsider, a foreigner, a man who did not belong to the land in which he dwelt. This identity as a stranger and sojourner would become one of the defining characteristics of the Hebrew people throughout their history.

After four hundred years in Egypt, the Hebrews were recognizable as a distinct people group (Exodus 1:19). The Egyptians could identify them by their customs, their language, and their appearance. The Philistines in Canaan used the term *"Hebrews"* to describe them (1 Samuel 29:3). Jonah identified himself as *"a Hebrew"* when questioned by the sailors on the storm-tossed ship (Jonah 1:9), and centuries later the apostle Paul was still claiming the same identity with pride: *"a Hebrew of Hebrews"* (Philippians 3:5).

Strictly speaking, if the Hebrews are *"descendants of Eber,"* then the term could encompass more than just Abraham's line. Other descendants of Eber who are not part of the covenant line could technically be considered Hebrews as well (Genesis 11:10-26). But in practice, both in Scripture and in common usage, Hebrew has always referred to the people descended from Abraham through Isaac and Jacob.

Who Are the Israelites?

The Israelites are the physical descendants of Abraham through Isaac and Jacob. When God changed Jacob's name to Israel in Genesis 32:28, a dramatic moment that occurred during Jacob's all-night wrestling match with the Angel of the Lord at the brook Jabbok, his sons and all their descendants became the "children of Israel" or "Israelites." The name Israel itself carries profound meaning. It is typically understood to mean "he struggles with God" or "God prevails," and both meanings are appropriate to Jacob's experience and to the history of the nation that would bear his name. Israel has been a nation that has struggled with God, and God has prevailed in that struggle again and again.

Jacob had twelve sons, and those twelve sons became the founders of the twelve tribes. In the Old Testament, the word Israelite is used frequently to describe any member of the covenant nation (Exodus 5:19; Leviticus 24:10; Nehemiah 9:2). In the New Testament, Jesus called Nathanael an *"Israelite"* (John 1:47), and Paul identified himself the same way (Romans 11:1). The word carries both an ethnic and a spiritual dimension. To be an Israelite was to belong to the nation with whom God had established His covenant.

The Israelites were the recipients of extraordinary privileges and responsibilities. They received the Mosaic Covenant at Sinai (Exodus 19-24), which defined their relationship with God in terms of law, worship, and national identity. They received the Palestinian, or Land, Covenant (Deuteronomy 29:1-29), which specified the conditions for their possession of the Promised Land. They received the Davidic Covenant (1 Chronicles 17:11-14), which promised an eternal dynasty culminating in the Messiah. And they received the promise of a New Covenant (Jeremiah 31:31, 33), which would one day replace the old covenant with a new one written on the heart rather than on tablets of stone. This New Covenant was extended, by the grace of God, to include anyone, Jew and Gentile alike, who has faith in Jesus Christ (Romans 10:12).

But the New Testament introduces an important distinction that has profound implications for the Middle East conflict and for the church's understanding of Israel. Jesus called Nathanael an Israelite *"indeed"* (John 1:47), suggesting that being an Israelite by birth was not the same as being an Israelite in the fullest spiritual sense. The word translated "indeed" carries the sense of "truly" or "genuinely." Nathanael was a man in whom there was no deceit, no pretense, no gap between his ethnic identity and his spiritual reality. He was the real thing.

When Jesus met Zacchaeus, a tax collector who was ethnically an Israelite but had been living in a way that made him a pariah in his own community, He declared, *"Today salvation has come to this house, because this man, too, is a son of Abraham"* (Luke 19:9). Zacchaeus had always been a physical descendant of Abraham. But on that day, through his encounter with Jesus, he became a spiritual son of Abraham as well. Paul developed this theme further, teaching that *"those who have faith are children of Abraham"* (Galatians 3:7). The implication is profound: true membership in God's covenant people is defined not by bloodline alone but by faith. Nicodemus, one of Israel's most respected leaders, had to be told that he needed to be "born again" (John 3:3). His ethnic credentials were impeccable, but without the new birth, they were insufficient.

God promised to bless the Israelites as they kept the Law of Moses. Through the centuries, He used the Israelites in extraordinary ways. Paul summarized their privileges in one of the most powerful passages in his letter to the Romans:

> *"They are Israelites, and to them belong the adoption, the glory, the covenants, the giving*
> *of the law, the worship, and the promises. To them belong the patriarchs, and from their*
> *race, according to the flesh, is the Christ, who is God over all, blessed forever. Amen."*
> *(Romans 9:4-5, ESV)*

Notice the weight of what Paul is saying. The adoption as God's sons, the visible manifestation of God's glory, the covenants, the law, the temple worship, the messianic promises, the patriarchs, and, above all, Jesus Christ Himself, all of these came through Israel. The Israelites were not merely one nation among many. They were the nation through whom God chose to reveal Himself, record His Word, and bring His Son into the world. God also promised that through Abraham's lineage, all of humanity would be blessed (Genesis 12:3). Jesus Christ is the ultimate fulfillment of that universal promise.

Who Are the Jews?

This is where the terminology becomes particularly interesting. The word Jew does not appear in the Bible until relatively late. In the King James Version, it first appears in 2 Kings 16:6, and in most other translations, it does not show up until 2 Kings 25:25. In those early instances, the Hebrew word would likely be better translated as *"men of Judah."* The word becomes much more common in the books of Ezra, Nehemiah, and Esther, all of which were written after the Babylonian exile.

The reason for this timing is straightforward. After the ten northern tribes were exiled to Assyria and the southern kingdom was taken to Babylon, the tribe of Judah became the dominant surviving group. When the exiles returned to the Promised Land under Ezra and Nehemiah, Judah was the leading tribe in the restoration community. The word Jew developed as a shortening of the word Judah, and over time it came to refer not just to members of the tribe of Judah but to all Israelites, people from all twelve tribes.

So who was the first Jew? The answer depends on how you define the term. If by "Jew" you mean "Hebrew," then Abraham was the first Jew. If you mean "of the tribe of Judah," then Judah himself, Jacob's fourth son, was the first Jew. If you mean "the first person in the Bible to be referred to by that term," then the unnamed individuals in 2 Kings are the first Jews. In common usage today, when people speak of a "Jew," they generally mean a person who belongs to God's chosen people, descended from Abraham, Isaac, and Jacob. With that definition in mind, Abraham is rightly considered the first Jew.

Technically, a strict definition would note that Jews are Israelite Hebrews from the region of Judea. They descend from Abraham (a Hebrew), through Jacob (an Israelite), through Judah (a Jew). Under this narrow definition, not all Israelite Hebrews are Jews. After Solomon's death, the ten tribes of the Northern Kingdom were non-Judean Hebrew Israelites, while the two tribes of the Southern Kingdom were the Judean Hebrew Israelites. But in everyday conversation and in most biblical scholarship, the terms Jews, Israelites, and Hebrews are used interchangeably to refer to God's chosen people. For the purposes of this book, and for understanding the modern Middle East conflict, the common usage is sufficient.

Abraham's grandson Jacob's name was changed to "Israel" (Genesis 35:10), so Jacob and his descendants could be called the first "Israelites." Jacob's fourth son was named "Judah," and his descendants were called "Judahites" or "Judeans." Later, the name "Judean" was shortened to "Jew." This progression from Hebrew to Israelite to Jew traces the narrowing and refining of God's covenant people across the generations, from a broad ethnic identity to a specific tribal identity to a comprehensive national designation that would carry through the rest of history.

What Is a Gentile?

The word Gentile is an English translation of the Hebrew word "goyim", meaning "peoples" or "nations," and the Greek word ethne, meaning "nations" or "people groups." The Latin Vulgate translated these words as gentilis, which was carried into English as Gentile. In the simplest terms, a Gentile is anyone who is not a Jew.

It is worth noting that the word goyim is not inherently negative. In some Old Testament passages, the word is used simply to mean "nations" in a neutral sense. Even Israel itself is occasionally referred to as a goy (Exodus 19:6). But over time, particularly in the intertestamental period and into the first century, the term took on increasingly negative connotations in Jewish usage, becoming associated with paganism, spiritual ignorance, and ritual impurity.

From the Jewish perspective, particularly by the time of Jesus, Gentiles were often regarded as pagans who did not know the true God. Many Jews took such pride in their cultural and religious heritage that they viewed Gentiles as inherently unclean, calling them "dogs" and "the uncircumcision." Gentiles, along with the half-Gentile Samaritans, were enemies to be avoided (John 4:9; 18:28; Acts 10:28). A devout Jew would not enter the home of a Gentile, would not eat with a Gentile, and would undergo ritual purification after any contact with Gentile people or objects. The separation that God had intended as a testimony to the world had been transformed, in the hands of human pride, into a wall of contempt.

Jesus Himself acknowledged the common association between Gentiles and paganism in His Sermon on the Mount, but He did so in a way that challenged Jewish complacency rather than reinforcing it. He pointed out that even Gentiles greet their own people warmly and pray with many words (Matthew 5:47; 6:7). The implication was not that Gentiles were hopeless, but that God expected more from His covenant people. If even pagans could show kindness to their friends, what distinguished Israel? The answer should have been a love and holiness so extraordinary that it drew the nations toward God, not a self-righteous exclusivism that pushed them away.

More importantly, Jesus came to offer salvation to all people, Jew and Gentile alike. The prophet Isaiah had predicted this centuries earlier, declaring that the Messiah would bring justice to the Gentiles and would be a light to the nations (Isaiah 42:1, 6). Simeon, the elderly priest who held the infant Jesus in the temple, recognized the child as *"a light for revelation to the Gentiles, and the glory of your people Israel"* (Luke 2:32). Notice the order: a light to the Gentiles first, and then the glory of Israel. The universal mission preceded and encompassed the national blessing.

In Mark 7:26, Jesus helped a Gentile woman, a Syrophoenician, who pleaded for her daughter's freedom from a demon. The exchange between Jesus and this woman is one of the most theologically dense conversations in the Gospels. Jesus initially appeared to refuse her request, saying, *"First let the children eat all they want, for it is not right to take the children's bread and toss it to the dogs"* (Mark 7:27). The woman's response was remarkable: *"Lord, even the dogs under the table eat the children's crumbs"* (Mark 7:28). She was not offended by Jesus' language. She understood the priority of Israel in God's plan and was willing to receive even the overflow of blessing that fell from the covenant table. Jesus, moved by her faith, healed her daughter immediately. This moment foreshadowed the universal scope of His mission and demonstrated that Gentile faith could be as genuine and powerful as anything found in Israel.

In a striking detail, both Jews and Gentiles are implicated in the death of Jesus. The Jewish religious leaders arrested Him, but it was a Roman, a Gentile, who sentenced Him to death, and Roman soldiers who carried out the execution (Luke 18:32). The early church recognized this shared responsibility. In their prayer recorded in Acts 4, the apostles declared: *"Indeed Herod and Pontius Pilate met together with the Gentiles and the people of Israel in this city to conspire against your holy servant Jesus"* (Acts 4:27). The cross stands as the place where Jewish and Gentile guilt converge, and, mercifully, where Jewish and Gentile redemption is offered.

The Gentiles Enter the Story of Salvation

The conversion of Gentiles in the early church was initially met with astonishment. The event that shattered the barrier most dramatically was Peter's visit to the household of Cornelius, a Roman centurion stationed in Caesarea (Acts 10). Cornelius was a God-fearer, a Gentile who worshiped the God of Israel but had not fully converted to Judaism through circumcision. An angel appeared to Cornelius and instructed him to send for Peter. At the same time, God gave Peter a vision of a sheet descending from heaven filled with animals that Jewish dietary law classified as unclean. A voice said, *"Do not call anything impure that God has made clean"* (Acts 10:15). The vision came three times.

When Peter arrived at Cornelius's house and began to preach the Gospel, something unprecedented happened. The Holy Spirit fell upon everyone present, Jew and Gentile alike, and the Gentiles began speaking in tongues and praising God (Acts 10:44-46). The Jewish believers who had accompanied Peter were "astonished that the gift of the Holy Spirit had been poured out even on Gentiles" (Acts 10:45). Peter's conclusion was as simple as it was revolutionary: *"Surely no one can stand in the way of their being baptized with water. They have received the Holy Spirit just as we have"* (Acts 10:47).

This event was so significant that Peter was summoned to Jerusalem to explain himself to the Jewish Christian leadership. When he recounted what had happened, the response was historic: the Jewish believers in Jerusalem *"praised God, saying, 'So then, even to Gentiles God has granted repentance that leads to life'"* (Acts 11:18). That sentence, spoken in wonder, marks one of the most pivotal moments in the history of the church. The wall between Jew and Gentile, maintained for centuries by law, custom, and deep-seated prejudice, was beginning to crumble under the weight of grace.

As the Gospel continued to spread, entire Gentile communities responded with eagerness. In Pisidian Antioch, when the Gentiles heard the good news, *"they were glad and honored the word of the Lord; and all who were appointed for eternal life believed"* (Acts 13:48). The church at Antioch in Syria became the first major Gentile Christian community and served as the launching point for Paul's missionary journeys into the wider Mediterranean world. It was at Antioch that the disciples were first called *"Christians"* (Acts 11:26), a name that transcended the Jew-Gentile divide and identified believers by their relationship to Christ rather than by their ethnic heritage.

Paul and the Gospel for All Nations

No figure in the New Testament grappled more directly with the Jew-Gentile divide than the apostle Paul. As a Pharisee, Paul had been steeped in Jewish separatism. He described his former life in terms that leave no doubt about the intensity of his commitment to Jewish distinctiveness: *"Circumcised on the eighth day, of the people of Israel, of the tribe of Benjamin, a Hebrew of Hebrews; in regard to the law, a Pharisee; as for zeal, persecuting the church; as for righteousness based on the law, faultless"* (Philippians 3:5-6).

This was a man who had devoted his entire life to maintaining the boundary between Jew and Gentile, between the chosen and the unchosen, between the clean and the unclean. As a convert to Christ, he became the primary architect of a theology that held Jews and Gentiles together in one body under one Savior. His statement in Romans 1:16 serves as a thesis for his entire ministry:

> *"For I am not ashamed of the Gospel, because it is the power of God that brings salvation to everyone who believes: first to the Jew, then to the Gentile." (Romans 1:16)*

That phrase, "first to the Jew, then to the Gentile," is not a statement of superiority. It is a statement of chronology and covenant priority. The Gospel message was first revealed to the Jewish people because the Messiah had come through their lineage, had been promised through their prophets, and had been anticipated through their sacrificial system. It was natural, even necessary, that the good news be proclaimed first to the people who had been prepared over centuries to receive it.

The Jews are God's chosen people (Deuteronomy 7:6-7). Through them, God demonstrated His love and holiness to the world. They were given the adoption as sons, the divine glory, the covenants, the law, the temple worship, and the promises (Romans 9:4-5). Through the seed of Abraham, all peoples on earth would be blessed (Acts 3:25; Genesis 22:18). That promised blessing came through Jesus Christ, as Paul explained: *"Now to Abraham and his seed were the promises made. He saith not, And to seeds, as of many; but as of one, And to thy seed, which is Christ"* (Galatians 3:16). The singular "seed" is critical. The promise was not made to Abraham's descendants in general, but to one specific descendant: Jesus Christ.

In His public ministry, Jesus focused His efforts on the Jewish people. He was the Jewish Messiah, sent to *"strengthen Judah and save the tribes of Joseph"* (Zechariah 10:6). He told His disciples during their initial mission, *"Do not go among the Gentiles or enter any town of the Samaritans. Go rather to the lost sheep of Israel"* (Matthew 10:5-6). He predicted that *"repentance for the forgiveness of sins will be preached in His name to all nations, beginning at Jerusalem"* (Luke 24:47). The Gospel of the kingdom was a blessing destined for the whole world, but it was launched from Jerusalem, among the Jews, by Jewish apostles.

We see this pattern clearly in Paul's missionary journeys. In every new city he entered, his first stop was the synagogue, where he preached to the Jewish community. When the Jews in Pisidian Antioch rejected the message, Paul and Barnabas made a statement that would define the rest of the apostolic mission: *"We had to speak the word of God to you first. Since you reject it and do not consider yourselves worthy of eternal life, we now turn to the Gentiles"* (Acts 13:46). This was not an emotional outburst. It was a theological principle enacted in real time. The Gospel had been offered to those who were first in line. When they refused it, the door opened wider.

The turning to the Gentiles did not mean the abandonment of the Jews. Throughout his missionary career, Paul continued to preach in synagogues in every city he visited. God's desire for the salvation of all the world never narrowed (John 3:16-18; 1 Timothy 2:4). Paul himself agonized over the unbelief of his own people, writing to the Romans: *"I have great sorrow and unceasing anguish in my heart. For I could wish that I myself were cursed and cut off from Christ for the sake of my people, those of my own race, the people of Israel"* (Romans 9:2-4). This is not the language of a man who had given up on the Jews. It is the language of a man whose love for his people was so intense that he would trade his own salvation for theirs if he could.

In Romans 11, Paul developed the relationship between Jewish unbelief and Gentile inclusion with the extended metaphor of an olive tree. The natural branches (the Jewish people) had been broken off because of unbelief, and wild branches (the Gentile believers) had been grafted in to share in the nourishing root. But Paul warned the Gentile believers against arrogance: *"Do not be arrogant, but tremble. For if God did not spare the natural branches, he will not spare you either"* (Romans 11:20-21). Gentile believers were beneficiaries of Jewish failure, not replacements for the Jewish people.

Then Paul revealed a mystery that has profound implications for the Middle East and for the future of the world: *"Israel has experienced a hardening in part until the full number of the Gentiles has come in, and in this way all Israel will be saved"* (Romans 11:25-26). Whatever one's interpretation of this passage, and Christians have debated it for centuries, it is clear that Paul did not consider the story of Israel to be finished. The God who had called Abraham, who had established His covenant with Isaac and Jacob, who had brought His people through exile and restoration, had not written the final chapter. There is a future for Israel in God's plan, and it is a future of salvation.

Three Truths About Salvation and the Great Divide

Paul's teaching on Jews and Gentiles in the plan of salvation carries three truths that are essential for understanding the Middle East conflict and the Christian's responsibility within it.

First, God did not stop saving Jews in order to save Gentiles. The inclusion of the Gentiles in the plan of salvation was never a replacement for Israel. Paul made this point emphatically in Romans 11, using the image of the olive tree. The Gentile believers were branches grafted into the tree, not a new tree planted in place of the old one. God continues to desire the salvation of Jewish people, and the story of Israel in God's plan is not over. Any theology that teaches that the church has permanently replaced Israel in God's purposes must reckon with Paul's clear statement that *"God's gifts and his call are irrevocable"* (Romans 11:29). What God has promised to Israel, He will fulfill.

Second, Jews are neither better nor worse than Gentiles. All human beings need a Savior, and in Christ, all stand on equal spiritual ground. Paul wrote to the Colossians, *"You have put on the new self, which is being renewed in knowledge in the image of its Creator. Here there is no Gentile or Jew, circumcised or uncircumcised, barbarian, Scythian, slave or free, but Christ is all, and is in all"* (Colossians 3:10-11). The believing Gentile is just as welcome in the family of God as the believing Jew. The Jewish believer is just as secure in salvation as the born-again Gentile. At the foot of the cross, every human distinction of heritage, ethnicity, social status, and cultural superiority is leveled.

Third, salvation comes the same way to both Jews and Gentiles. It is for *"everyone who believes"* (Romans 1:16). Jesus is the only way of salvation (Acts 4:12; John 14:6), regardless of heritage, ethnicity, or national identity. Paul declared, *"I have declared to both Jews and Greeks that they must turn to God in repentance and have faith in our Lord Jesus"* (Acts 20:21). There is no Jewish path to God and no Gentile path to God. There is one path: Jesus Christ. Galatians 3:26-28 makes it as plain as language allows: *"So in Christ Jesus you are all children of God through faith, for all of you who were baptized into Christ have clothed yourselves with Christ. There is neither Jew nor Gentile, neither slave nor free, nor is there male and female, for you are all one in Christ Jesus."* All must come to Jesus in faith for salvation, and all are equally accepted by Him when they do.

The Dividing Wall Destroyed

Perhaps the most powerful statement of what Christ accomplished between Jew and Gentile comes in Paul's letter to the Ephesians. Writing to a Gentile church, he reminded them of where they had come from and what Christ had accomplished:

"Remember that at that time you were separate from Christ, excluded from citizenship in Israel and foreigners to the covenants of the promise, without hope and without God in the world. But now in Christ Jesus you who once were far away have been brought near by the blood of Christ. For he himself is our peace, who has made the two groups one and has destroyed the barrier, the dividing wall of hostility." (Ephesians 2:12-14)

That "dividing wall" is not merely a metaphor. In the Jerusalem temple, there was a literal stone barrier, called the **soreg**, that separated the Court of the Gentiles from the inner courts. Archaeologists have recovered fragments of the warning signs that were posted on that wall. The inscription, written in Greek, read: *"No foreigner may enter within the barrier and enclosure around the temple. Anyone who is caught doing so will have himself to blame for his ensuing death."* Gentiles could come to the temple, but they could come no further than the outer court. The wall said, in the most literal terms possible: *"This far and no further. You are not one of us."*

The Soreg was a low stone barrier or railing in the Second Temple in Jerusalem that separated the Court of the Gentiles from the inner courts of the Temple, which were reserved for Jews. This partition marked the boundary beyond which Gentiles were not permitted to pass. Historical sources indicate that warning inscriptions were placed along this barrier stating that any non-Jew who crossed it would be responsible for their own death.

The Soreg is significant theologically because it symbolized the division between Jews and Gentiles in temple worship. In the New Testament, the apostle Paul uses this imagery when he explains that through Christ the barrier separating Jews and Gentiles has been removed. Ephesians 2:14 (KJV) states, *"For he is our peace, who hath made both one, and hath broken down the middle wall of partition between us."* Thus, what was once a physical and spiritual boundary in the Temple becomes a powerful symbol of how redemption in Christ unites all people into one body before God.

Paul, who was falsely accused of bringing a Gentile named Trophimus past that barrier (Acts 21:28-29), an accusation that nearly cost him his life, understood the power of the image better than anyone. When he wrote that Christ had *"destroyed the barrier, the dividing wall of hostility,"* he was describing something his original readers could visualize with absolute clarity. Christ did not lower the wall. He did not cut a door in it. He destroyed it. The separation between Jew and Gentile that had been maintained by law, custom, architecture, and centuries of accumulated prejudice was demolished by the cross.

This does not mean that the distinction between Jew and Gentile has ceased to exist in every sense. Paul himself continued to identify as a Jew and to recognize the unique covenant history of the Jewish people. The promises made to Abraham, Isaac, and Jacob regarding the land, the descendants, and the blessing have not been revoked (Romans 11:29). But the relationship between Jew and Gentile has been fundamentally transformed by the cross. What was once a wall of hostility has become, in Christ, a ground of reconciliation.

The Divide and the Middle East

Why does this theological material matter for understanding the Middle East conflict? Because the division of humanity into Jews and Gentiles is not merely a historical category from the ancient world. It is a living reality that shapes national identities, territorial claims, and religious convictions in the region to this day.

The Jewish claim to the land of Israel is rooted in the covenant promises made to Abraham, Isaac, and Jacob, promises that were given specifically to the Jewish people as defined by their descent from these patriarchs. The Arab nations, many of whom trace their ancestry to Ishmael and Esau, hold competing claims to the same territory based on their own understanding of Abrahamic heritage. The Christian world, called to carry the Gospel to all nations, stands in the middle of this tension, bearing a message that transcends ethnic and national boundaries while also affirming the historical reality of God's covenant with Israel.

Paul's teaching offers a framework that neither erases the distinction between Jew and Gentile nor allows that distinction to become a barrier to the Gospel. God's promises to Israel remain valid, but they find their ultimate fulfillment in Christ. God's invitation to the Gentiles is genuine and complete, but it does not nullify the unique role Israel plays in the unfolding of prophetic history. The olive tree stands. The natural branches have not been permanently discarded. And the wild branches that have been grafted in have no grounds for boasting.

As we turn in the next chapter to the historical roots of the Israeli-Arab conflict, we will see how the ancient family divisions we have traced, Ishmael and Isaac, Esau and Jacob, the twelve tribes and their scattered descendants, have produced a modern reality that the world's politicians struggle to understand and its diplomats fail to resolve. But we will also see that the God who made promises to both Isaac and Ishmael, who wept over Jerusalem and died for the world, has not abandoned His plan. The great divide between Jew and Gentile is real, but it is not the final word. The final word belongs to the cross.

Paul himself, a Hebrew of Hebrews, a Pharisee of the strictest order, a man who had once persecuted the church with murderous zeal, became the living proof that God's grace could bridge any divide. If the God who saved Saul of Tarsus and transformed him into the apostle to the Gentile world could accomplish that miracle, then there is no division, no animosity, no ancient hatred so deep that it lies beyond His reach. That conviction is not naive optimism. It is the testimony of Scripture, and it is the foundation on which every Christian response to the Middle East conflict must be built.

Chapter 10

ROOTS OF BLOOD: THE ISRAELI-ARAB CONFLICT

"And he will be a wild man; his hand will be against every man, and every man's hand against him; and he shall dwell in the presence of all his brethren." (Genesis 16:12, KJV)

We have now traced the biblical story from Abraham's call through the covenant promises, through the births of Ishmael and Isaac, through Jacob and Esau, through the twelve tribes and their scattered history, and through the great theological divide between Jew and Gentile. At every stage, we have seen how choices made by individuals and nations set in motion consequences that would echo across centuries. Now we arrive at the place where all those threads converge: the roots of the Israeli-Arab conflict.

This is the chapter where ancient promises and ancient grievances meet. The conflict that dominates our headlines, that fills our news feeds with images of destruction and displacement, that has frustrated every peace process and defied every diplomatic solution for more than a century, did not begin with the establishment of the modern state of Israel in 1948. It did not begin with the Balfour Declaration in 1917. It did not even begin with the rise of Zionism in the late nineteenth century. The roots of this conflict go all the way back to a tent in the ancient Near East, where a man named Abraham, struggling with the tension between God's promise and his own impatience, fathered two sons who would become the patriarchs of two peoples locked in an enmity that has never been resolved by human effort.

In this chapter, we will examine the theological, genealogical, and historical roots of the conflict. We will look at the role of Ishmael and Esau, the two primary patriarchs of the Arab nations. We will examine the competing claims of the Bible and the Koran. We will trace God's two land covenants and their implications for the modern territorial dispute. And we will see how the prophets of the Old Testament described, with astonishing precision, the very dynamics that we watch unfolding in the Middle East today.

Abraham's Three Faiths

One of the most remarkable facts about Abraham is that three of the world's major religions claim him as a founding figure. Judaism, Christianity, and Islam all honor Abraham as a patriarch, and all three trace significant elements of their identity back to his story. This shared heritage might seem like a natural starting point for peace. If Jews, Christians, and Muslims all revere the same ancient father, should that not provide common ground for reconciliation?

The answer, as history has demonstrated repeatedly, is no. The reason is not that these three faiths share too little in common, but that they disagree on matters too fundamental to be papered over by a shared ancestor. The disagreements concern the identity of the son of promise, the nature of God Himself, the authority of Scripture, and the path of salvation. These are not minor theological details. They are the load-bearing walls of each faith system, and they produce radically different conclusions about who has a rightful claim to the land, to the covenant, and to the future.

Abraham is indispensable to Christianity, but for a far different reason than he is to Judaism or Islam. Christians hold to the same historical account as the Jews: Abraham and Sarah were given the son of promise, Isaac. Through Isaac came Jacob, and through Jacob came the twelve tribes of Israel. But Christianity makes a conclusion that goes further. Christians view God's interaction and covenant with Abraham as a divine plan leading to the first coming of Jesus Christ, an appearance that would see Him becoming the sacrificial Lamb of God to cover the sins of mankind. Abraham's willingness to offer Isaac on Mount Moriah (Genesis 22) is understood as a prophetic picture of God the Father offering His own Son on the cross. The ram caught in the thicket, provided by God as a substitute for Isaac, foreshadows Christ, the Lamb of God who would take away the sin of the world (John 1:29).

Abraham in Islam

Abraham's role in Islam is fundamentally different from that which he plays in either Christianity or Judaism. Arab Muslims trace their lineage back to Abraham through Ishmael. The Koran teaches that Ishmael, not Isaac, was the son through whom God's covenant would be fulfilled. The Koranic account of Abraham is not as extensive as the Hebrew account. It dwells primarily on a struggle between Abraham and his father over idol worship. The Koranic Abraham tries to convince his father not to worship things that cannot see, hear, feel, taste, or smell. When his father refuses, Abraham leaves to become a true worshiper of Allah, and in return for his faithfulness, Allah gives him two sons, Jacob and Ishmael, with Ishmael being the one whom Abraham offered on the altar to Allah.

According to Islamic tradition, before Ishmael was weaned, Abraham took the child and his mother Hagar to Mecca and left them there, trusting that Allah would provide for them. Abraham later had a dream instructing him to sacrifice his only son, Ishmael. Before he could carry out the sacrifice, God stopped him. Abraham subsequently returned to Mecca on various occasions and, together with Ishmael, built a "House for pilgrimage of men" devoted to Allah. This structure is identified in Islamic tradition as the Kaaba, the cube-shaped building in Mecca that is the most sacred site in Islam and the focal point of the hajj pilgrimage.

The Islamic holiday Qurbani Id, also known as Id Al-Adha or the Sacrifice Festival, celebrates Abraham's willingness to sacrifice Ishmael. Muslims observe this great feast on the tenth day of the last month of the Muslim year. According to their doctrinal framework, this day honors not the offering of Isaac, as the Bible records, but the offering of Ishmael. This single discrepancy is not an isolated textual difference. It is a fundamental reorientation of the entire Abrahamic narrative, and its implications for the Middle East conflict are enormous.

The Bible and the Koran: Two Incompatible Claims

This disagreement over Isaac and Ishmael is one of hundreds of differences between the Bible and the Koran, and these differences concern the most consequential themes in all of theology: the nature of God, the identity of Christ, and the means of salvation. Both the Bible and the Koran claim divine inspiration, but the claims they make are mutually exclusive on these central issues. They cannot both be right.

The question, then, is one of authority. If the Bible is the revelation of God, then Christianity is the true religion, and the covenant promises regarding the land belong to the descendants of Isaac and Jacob. If the Koran is the revelation of God, then Islam is the genuine system, and Ishmael's descendants hold the prior claim. Unlike the Koran, the Holy Bible is composed of a remarkable internal unity. Although recorded by approximately forty inspired human writers over a period of some fifteen hundred years, it contains an astonishing consistency of purpose and doctrine. It includes hundreds of detailed prophecies that were later fulfilled with precision. Although challenged by the most renowned skeptics across the centuries, the Bible has been found to be without error, and it continues to demonstrate its own credibility as time passes and as archaeological discoveries confirm its historical claims.

One additional contrast deserves attention. The Bible encourages believers to love their enemies (Matthew 5:44). The Koran, while containing passages that speak of mercy and compassion, also contains passages that have been historically interpreted to promote conversion by force and jihad, or "holy war." The Bible records that Abraham was willing to offer Isaac. The Koran implies that Abraham was willing to offer Ishmael. The issue, at its simplest, is this: Which volume is God's? The answer to that question determines everything else.

For the purposes of understanding the Middle East conflict, this theological divergence has enormous practical consequences. When both sides believe God is on their side, and both sides appeal to ancient texts to justify their claims, the possibility of compromise becomes extraordinarily difficult. This is why the conflict has defied every diplomatic solution for over a century. It is not primarily a dispute over land or resources or national borders. It is a dispute over revelation, over which book carries the authority of God, and therefore over which people hold the divine mandate to the Promised Land.

Ishmael: The First Root of the Conflict

We examined the story of Ishmael in detail in earlier chapters, but it is essential to revisit its significance specifically in the context of the conflict. In Genesis 16, Sarah, believing herself to be barren after ten years of waiting for God's promise of a son, gave her Egyptian handmaid Hagar to Abraham as a secondary wife. This was consistent with the customs of the ancient Near East, but it was not consistent with the promise God had made. Both Abraham and Sarah demonstrated a lack of faith in this arrangement, because God had already specified that the son of promise would come through Sarah herself (Genesis 12).

Hagar conceived and bore Ishmael. Rather than remaining in submission to her mistress, Hagar began to display contempt for Sarah. In the ancient world, few women were more despised than those who were barren, and Hagar's fertility gave her a sense of superiority over the wife she was supposed to serve. Sarah responded harshly, and the pregnant handmaid fled into the wilderness, a decision that meant almost certain death for a young pregnant woman in the desert.

There, in one of the most remarkable encounters in Scripture, Hagar had a conversation with the Angel of the Lord, the first recorded conversation between God and a woman since Eve. God did not abandon Hagar. He found her in her desperation, spoke to her with tenderness, and gave her both instructions and promises. He told her to return to Sarah, and He gave her four prophecies concerning her son Ishmael and his descendants.

"And the angel of the Lord said unto her, I will multiply thy seed exceedingly, that it shall not be numbered for multitude. And the angel of the Lord said unto her, Behold, thou art with child, and shalt bear a son, and shalt call his name Ishmael; because the Lord hath heard thy affliction. And he will be a wild man; his hand will be against every man, and every man's hand against him; and he shall dwell in the presence of all his brethren." (Genesis 16:10-12, KJV)

Hagar responded by giving God a name that no other person in Scripture gives Him: *"El-Roi,"* the God who sees (Genesis 16:13). In her darkest moment, alone in the wilderness, pregnant and desperate, Hagar discovered that the God of Abraham was also the God who saw her. This is a detail worth pausing over. God's covenant was with Isaac's line, but His compassion extended to Hagar and Ishmael. The same God who chose one family for a specific covenantal purpose also cared for those outside that covenant line. This dual reality, God's particular election and His universal compassion, runs throughout the entire biblical narrative and is essential for understanding the Middle East conflict with a Christian heart.

These prophecies concerning Ishmael have been fulfilled with remarkable precision. Today there are more than twenty Arab states with a combined population of hundreds of millions, spanning 5.3 million square miles of oil-rich territory. The promise that Ishmael's descendants would be multiplied *"exceedingly"* has been kept. The description of Ishmael as a *"wild man,"* a phrase that speaks to fierce independence and warrior culture, characterizes the Bedouin tradition and the broader Arab martial heritage. The prophecy that *"his hand will be against every man, and every man's hand against him"* describes the perpetual cycle of aggression and retaliation that has defined Arab-Israeli relations, particularly since the establishment of the modern state of Israel in 1948. And the promise that Ishmael would *"dwell in the presence of all his brethren"* has been fulfilled in the geographic reality that Arab nations surround Israel on virtually every side.

God later elaborated on His promises for Ishmael when He established the covenant of circumcision with Abraham. In Genesis 17:20, God told Abraham directly: *"And as for Ishmael, I have heard thee: Behold, I have blessed him, and will make him fruitful, and will multiply him exceedingly; twelve princes shall he beget, and I will make him a great nation."* This is a genuine promise from the Lord God, Jehovah, and He has faithfully kept it.

But in the very next verse, God made the critical distinction that lies at the heart of the conflict: *"But my covenant will I establish with Isaac, which Sarah shall bear unto thee"* (Genesis 17:21). The blessing of Ishmael was real. The covenant with Isaac was exclusive. God blessed Ishmael, but He covenanted with Isaac. The land, the law, the priesthood, the temple, the monarchy, the prophets, and the Messiah were all channeled through Isaac, Jacob, and the nation of Israel. This is not a statement of ethnic superiority. It is a statement of covenantal specificity. God chose a particular line through which to accomplish a particular purpose, and that choice, while it does not diminish the value or dignity of those outside the covenant line, does establish a priority that Scripture never reverses.

Ironically, while the Bible offers genuine promises of blessing to the descendants of Ishmael, the Koran offers no such promises to the descendants of Isaac and Jacob. To the contrary, the most extreme interpretations of Islamic theology require that the seed of Abraham descended from Isaac and Jacob be subdued or destroyed. The Bible says, *"I will bless Ishmael."* The Koran's harshest voices say, *"Destroy the children of Isaac."* The asymmetry is striking and has direct consequences for the dynamics of the modern conflict.

Esau: The Second Root of the Conflict

If Ishmael represents the first root of the conflict, Esau represents the second. Unlike Ishmael and Isaac, who were half-brothers born to different mothers, Esau and Jacob were full brothers, twins born to Isaac and Rebekah. Before they were even born, God spoke a prophecy over them that would shape the rest of biblical history: *"Two nations are in your womb, and two peoples from within you will be separated; one people will be stronger than the other, and the older will serve the younger"* (Genesis 25:23). From the very beginning, it was clear that Esau, the firstborn, would serve Jacob, the second-born. The divine purpose was established before either child had done anything good or bad.

Esau, as the firstborn, was entitled to inherit the double portion of his father's inheritance and, more importantly, the covenantal role through which God would continue to fulfill the Abrahamic promises. But Esau did not want to be used of God to enact His program. In a moment of hunger and short-sightedness that the author of Hebrews would later describe as profane (Hebrews 12:16), Esau sold his covenantal status to Jacob for a bowl of lentil stew (Genesis 25:33-34). The text adds a detail that is more devastating than any editorial comment: *"So Esau despised his birthright"* (Genesis 25:34). He did not merely trade it. He despised it. He treated the covenant promise of God as something of less value than a single meal.

Jacob, for all his flaws, and they were many, wanted desperately to be in the center of God's plan. Later, with the help of his mother Rebekah's deception, Jacob disguised himself as Esau and received the patriarchal blessing from his aging, nearly blind father Isaac (Genesis 27). The blessing, once spoken, could not be recalled. When Esau discovered what had happened, his reaction was volcanic:

> *"And Esau hated Jacob because of the blessing wherewith his father blessed him: and Esau said in his heart, The days of mourning for my father are at hand; then will I slay my brother Jacob." (Genesis 27:41, KJV)*

That hatred did not die with Esau. It was passed down through generations like a genetic disease of the soul. Esau became the father of the Edomites, who settled in the mountainous region south of the Dead Sea, in the southern part of present-day Jordan (Genesis 25:30; 36:9, 43). The Edomites intermarried with the Ishmaelites, beginning with Esau himself, who married one of Ishmael's daughters (Genesis 28:9). This merging of the two lines of Abraham's dispossessed descendants created a combined heritage of grievance and hostility toward the children of Jacob that has never fully dissipated.

At one point, Jacob and Esau appeared to reconcile. In Genesis 33:1-4, when Jacob returned from his years with Laban, Esau ran to meet him, embraced him, fell on his neck, and kissed him, and they both wept. It is a moment of genuine tenderness. But the reconciliation did not last. The enmity between their descendants resumed and intensified over the centuries.

When Moses led the Israelites out of Egypt and requested peaceful passage through Edomite territory, the response was hostility: *"Thou shalt not pass through me, lest I come out with the sword against thee"* (Numbers 20:18). The Israelites asked politely. They promised to stay on the highway, not to touch the fields or vineyards, not to drink from the wells without paying. Edom refused and came out with a large army. Israel was forced to turn away and take a longer route. The blood of Esau could not tolerate the passage of the blood of Jacob, even when that passage was peaceful.

The treachery deepened when Jerusalem fell to Babylon in 586 BC. Rather than showing compassion to their kinsmen in the hour of their greatest catastrophe, the Edomites betrayed Jewish refugees into the hands of the Babylonians and openly rejoiced over the destruction of Jerusalem. The prophet Obadiah reserved some of the harshest language in all of Scripture for Edom's behavior: *"On the day you stood aloof while strangers carried off his wealth and foreigners entered his gates and cast lots for Jerusalem, you were like one of them. You should not gloat over your brother in the day of his misfortune"* (Obadiah 11-12). Ezekiel likewise condemned Edom's "perpetual hatred" and their eagerness to profit from Israel's suffering (Ezekiel 35:1-9).

The Arab states of today are descendants of either Ishmael or Esau, and in many cases both, due to centuries of intermarriage. The root of the present-day conflict begins with these two individuals and the bitterness they passed to their children. Not only is there Ishmael's resentment toward Isaac, but added to it is Esau's hatred toward Jacob. These two streams of grievance merged into a single river of animosity that has flowed through the centuries and shows no sign of drying up on its own.

God's Two Land Covenants

To understand the territorial dimension of the conflict, we need to distinguish between two covenants God made concerning the land. This distinction between title and possession is one of the most important, and most frequently misunderstood, concepts in the entire biblical framework for the Middle East.

The first is the Abrahamic Covenant, in which God gave the land of Canaan to Abraham's descendants through Isaac and Jacob in perpetuity (Genesis 12; 15; 17). This was an unconditional grant based on God's sovereign choice and Abraham's obedience. In Genesis 15, God formalized this covenant in a dramatic ceremony. Abraham was instructed to cut several animals in half and arrange the pieces in two rows, creating a path between them. In ancient Near Eastern covenant practice, both parties to an agreement would walk between the pieces, symbolizing that they would suffer the fate of the animals if they broke the covenant. But in this case, only God, represented by a smoking firepot and a blazing torch, passed between the pieces (Genesis 15:17). Abraham did not walk. The covenant was unilateral. God was binding Himself, and Himself alone, to this promise. The land grant does not depend on Israel's obedience. It depends on God's faithfulness.

God reiterated this promise to Isaac (Genesis 26:3-5), to Jacob (Genesis 28:13-15), and again in Genesis 35:12: *"The land I gave to Abraham and Isaac I also give to you, and I will give this land to your descendants after you."* Notice how God progressively narrowed the definition of the heirs: from Abraham to Isaac to Jacob to Jacob's twelve sons, who became the nation of Israel. Jacob and his family temporarily moved to Egypt because of a famine in Canaan but remained there four hundred years and became slaves of the Egyptians, then were brought back to conquer Canaan as God had foretold, establishing them as the heirs of God's promises to Abraham (Genesis 15:13-14). Thereafter, Canaan became known as the land of Israel, a title Scripture confers upon the territory more than thirty times.

The second covenant, outlined in Deuteronomy 28-30, defined the conditions under which Israel would enjoy possession of the land. This Land Covenant promised that Israel would become the preeminent nation on earth if the people obeyed God (Deuteronomy 28:1, 13), but warned that many curses would befall them if they were disobedient (Deuteronomy 28:15-37), including exile from the land (Deuteronomy 28:38-57). The covenant warned further that if temporary exile did not restore the Jews to obedience, they would suffer worldwide dispersion and persecution (Deuteronomy 28:58-68).

It is essential to understand the distinction between title and possession. Under the Abrahamic Covenant, the Jewish people hold permanent title to the land. Under the Land Covenant of Deuteronomy, their possession of the land is conditioned on obedience. The Jews have lost possession of the land multiple times throughout history: through the Assyrian exile, the Babylonian exile, the Roman destruction of Jerusalem in 70 AD, and the nearly two-thousand-year diaspora that followed. But they have never lost their God-given title. Nowhere in Scripture does God revoke the land grant He made to Abraham. An owner can be evicted from his property. He can be exiled from his homeland. But if the deed is in his name, the property is still his.

Furthermore, God said the true heirs to the promises would be slaves in a foreign land for four hundred years (Genesis 15:13). This never happened to the Arabs, but only to the Jews, who during this period of isolation in Egypt did not intermarry with non-Jews but became an identifiable ethnic group. They were then led by Moses and Joshua into the Promised Land. In sharp contrast, Ishmael's descendants intermarried freely with the Midianites (Judges 8:1, 12, 22, 24) and with the descendants of Esau (Genesis 28:9), who in turn intermarried with Hittites (Genesis 26:34). The four hundred years of Egyptian isolation served as a crucible that forged the Jewish people into a distinct nation, set apart for God's purposes. No comparable experience shaped the descendants of Ishmael. The Land Covenant ends with a remarkable prophecy and promise. After describing the curses that would befall a disobedient Israel, God declared that a day would come when He would restore His people:

"The Lord will restore you from captivity, and have compassion on you, and will gather you again from all the peoples where the Lord your God has scattered you.

If your outcasts are at the ends of the earth, from there the Lord your God will gather you, and from there He will bring you back. And the Lord your God will bring you into the land which your fathers possessed, and you shall possess it."

(Deuteronomy 30:3-5)

For almost two thousand years, the Jewish people wandered among the nations and suffered severe persecution, exactly as the Lord had prophesied in Deuteronomy 28. During all that time, the land lay desolate and cursed, as described in Deuteronomy 29. But in our time, God has begun to regather His people from the four corners of the earth, reestablish them in their land, and transform the wilderness into fruitfulness, as prophesied in Deuteronomy 30. The modern state of Israel, whatever one thinks of its politics, stands as tangible evidence that God keeps His word across millennia.

The Psalm 83 Conspiracy

One of the most striking prophetic passages relevant to the modern conflict is found in Psalm 83. The psalmist describes a united conspiracy whose stated aim is the annihilation of Israel as a nation:

"They have said, Come, and let us cut them off from being a nation; that the name of Israel may be no more in remembrance. For they have consulted together with one consent: they are confederate against thee: The tabernacles of Edom, and the Ishmaelites; of Moab, and the Hagarenes; Gebal, and Ammon, and Amalek; the Philistines with the inhabitants of Tyre; Assur also is joined with them." (Psalm 83:4-8, KJV)

Read that list carefully. Edom: the descendants of Esau, located in present-day southern Jordan. The Ishmaelites: the descendants of Ishmael, the broader Arab world. Moab and Ammon:

the descendants of Lot, also located in present-day Jordan. The Hagarenes: descendants of Hagar. Gebal: a region in modern Lebanon. Amalek: the ancient enemies of Israel from the Sinai region. The Philistines: inhabitants of the coastal plain, the area that roughly corresponds to modern Gaza. Tyre: a Phoenician city in modern Lebanon. Assur: Assyria, modern-day Iraq and parts of Syria.

It is no accident that modern Arab leaders have virtually paraphrased these ancient words in their campaigns against the state of Israel. The desire to eliminate Israel as a nation, to erase the name of the Jewish state from the map, is not a modern invention. It is the continuation of an enmity that the Bible described with prophetic precision thousands of years before it took its contemporary political form. The geographic correspondence between the ancient nations listed in Psalm 83 and the modern nations that surround and oppose Israel is striking and, for the student of Scripture, deeply significant.

But Psalm 83 does not end with the conspiracy. It ends with a prayer that the conspirators would be brought to shame so that they might seek the name of the Lord and know that He alone, *"whose name is Jehovah, is the Most High over all the earth"* (Psalm 83:18). Even in the midst of describing Israel's enemies, the psalmist prays not for their annihilation but for their conversion. This is a deeply Christian instinct, one that should shape how believers today pray for both Israelis and Palestinians, for both Jews and Arabs. The goal is not the destruction of Israel's enemies. The goal is that they would come to know the God of Israel.

Abraham's Other Descendants: The Wider Arab Heritage

The roots of the Arab peoples extend beyond Ishmael and Esau. After Sarah died at the age of 127, some twenty-eight years after giving birth to Isaac, Abraham took another wife named Keturah. The prophet Isaiah later declared Abraham and Sarah to be the father and mother of the

Hebrew people: *"Look to Abraham your father, and to Sarah who bore you"* (Isaiah 51:2). Keturah bore Abraham six more sons: Zimran, Jokshan, Medan, Midian, Ishbak, and Shuah (Genesis 25:1-2). These sons, like Ishmael before them, became the fathers of vast peoples throughout the Arabia-Mesopotamia region. The Midianites, who would later interact with Israel repeatedly throughout the period of the judges, descended from Abraham through Keturah.

The most significant detail in this account is how Abraham divided his estate. In accordance with God's instruction, Abraham gave all that he had, including the title to the land, to his son Isaac. To the sons of his concubines, Abraham gave gifts and sent them away *"eastward, unto the east country"* (Genesis 25:6). The prophet Jeremiah later confirmed that the eastern desert of Arabia became the domain of Abraham's non-Sarahite descendants, including Dedan, Midian, Joksham, Sheba, Kedar, and many others.

This estate division is not a minor detail. It establishes a biblical principle that applies directly to the modern territorial dispute. Abraham, under God's direction, made a deliberate choice about who would inherit the land and who would not. Isaac received the land. Everyone else received gifts and was directed elsewhere. This does not diminish the dignity or the blessing of Abraham's other descendants. God made specific promises to Ishmael and kept them faithfully. But the land itself was designated for Isaac's line, and that designation was reaffirmed to Jacob in Genesis 35:12.

When Isaac and Ishmael came together to bury their father Abraham in the cave of Machpelah (Genesis 25:9), there was a brief moment of family unity. Two brothers, separated by circumstance and destiny, stood side by side to honor the man who had fathered them both. Ishmael lived to be one hundred and thirty-seven years old, and Genesis records that *"he died in the presence of all his brethren"* (Genesis 25:17-18). The phrase echoes the original prophecy of Genesis 16:12. Even in death, Ishmael dwelt in the presence of his brothers. The proximity was permanent. The tension was permanent. And both, the Bible tells us, were part of the sovereign plan of God.

The Promise Before the Conflict

Before we close this chapter, it is important to step back and remember what came before the conflict. Before Ishmael's resentment, before Esau's hatred, before the Edomite betrayal and the Ishmaelite aggression, there was a promise. God said to Abraham:

"And I will make of thee a great nation, and I will bless thee, and make thy name great; and thou shalt be a blessing: And in thee shall all families of the earth be blessed." (Genesis 12:2-3, KJV)

The promise of the land was made to Abraham's *"seed,"* and as Christians, we understand that all these divine promises pointed ultimately to one descendant: Jesus Christ. Paul made this explicit: *"Now to Abraham and his seed were the promises made. He saith not, And to seeds, as of many; but as of one, And to thy seed, which is Christ"* (Galatians 3:16). The singular "seed" is the key. Not seeds, plural, as if referring to many descendants, but seed, singular, pointing to one Person.

Jesus Christ was the ultimate personal fulfillment of God's promise to Abraham. He was the seed planted within the national vehicle that Abraham fathered, and that seed would bless all nations. Jesus is also the thread that binds believers to every promise of God. Everything that God has pledged and portrayed in His eternal plan finds its center and its completion in Christ alone. He was and is the literal fulfillment of the ancient prophecy given to Adam in Genesis 3:15, that the seed of the woman would crush the head of the serpent.

This is the promise that stood before the conflict. And it is the promise that will stand after the conflict is resolved. The enmity between Ishmael and Isaac, between Esau and Jacob, between the Arab nations and Israel, is real and painful and ongoing. But it is not the deepest truth about the human story. The deepest truth is that God made a promise to bless all the families of the earth, and He has never broken a promise. The conflict does not nullify the promise. If anything, the ferocity of the conflict testifies to the significance of the promise. The enemy has always fought hardest against the plan of God that carries the greatest consequence for the world.

In the next chapter, we will trace how these ancient roots produced the modern conflict, from the rise of Zionism through the founding of the state of Israel, through the wars and intifadas and peace processes that have defined the last century, and into the devastating events of October 7, 2023, and their aftermath. The headlines will be more familiar, but the dynamics will be the same. The family of Abraham remains divided. But the God of Abraham remains faithful.

Chapter 11

TODAY'S HEADLINES, ANCIENT PROMISES

"For I will gather all nations against Jerusalem to battle . . . Then shall the LORD go forth, and fight against those nations, as when he fought in the day of battle." (Zechariah 14:2-3, KJV)

In the previous chapter, we traced the biblical roots of the Israeli-Arab conflict from the tents of Abraham to the prophetic visions of the Psalms. Now we make the leap from the ancient world to the modern one, a leap that is shorter than most people realize. The headlines that scroll across our screens today are the latest installments of a story that began nearly four thousand years ago. The players have changed, the weapons have evolved, and the political language has grown more sophisticated, but the underlying dynamics remain remarkably consistent with what Scripture described from the beginning.

In this chapter, we will trace the modern history of the conflict from the rise of Zionism in the late nineteenth century through the establishment of the state of Israel, the wars that followed, the ongoing Palestinian crisis, and the devastating events that have unfolded since October 7, 2023. At every stage, we will hold the modern events up to the light of the biblical framework we have built throughout this book, asking not just what happened but what it means in the context of God's covenantal purposes.

The Rise of Zionism and the British Mandate

Toward the end of the 1800s, Jewish communities across Europe faced intensifying persecution and anti-Semitism. Pogroms in Russia, legal discrimination in the Austro-Hungarian Empire, and the cultural anti-Semitism embedded in European intellectual life created an urgent question: How could the Jewish people secure a future free from the threat of annihilation? The answer, for a growing number of Jewish thinkers and activists, lay in the biblical Promised Land. The political movement known as Zionism emerged with the goal of establishing a Jewish homeland in Palestine.

Theodor Herzl, an Austro-Hungarian journalist, is widely regarded as the father of modern political Zionism. His 1896 pamphlet, *"Der Judenstaat"* ("The Jewish State"), argued that the only solution to the persistent persecution of Jews in Europe was the establishment of a sovereign Jewish state. The First Zionist Congress, convened by Herzl in Basel, Switzerland, in 1897, formally adopted the goal of creating a Jewish homeland in Palestine. From that point forward, Jewish immigration to the region, known as aliyah ("*ascent*"), began to accelerate.

From 1920 to 1947, the British Empire held a mandate over Palestine, a territory that included all of modern Israel and the areas now known as the West Bank and Gaza. During this period, Jewish immigration to the region increased steadily, creating tensions with the existing Arab population. The situation was complicated enormously by contradictory promises the British had made to different parties.

During World War I, the British convinced Arab leaders to revolt against the Ottoman Empire, which was allied with Germany, promising in return to support the establishment of an independent Arab state in the region, including Palestine. This arrangement, facilitated through correspondence between Sir Henry McMahon, the British High Commissioner in Egypt, and

Sharif Hussein of Mecca, is known as the Hussein-McMahon Correspondence of 1915-1916. Yet in 1917, Lord Arthur Balfour, then British Foreign Secretary, issued the Balfour Declaration, which announced the British Empire's support for the establishment of a Jewish national home in Palestine. On top of this, the Sykes-Picot Agreement of 1916 between Britain and France secretly divided the Ottoman territories into zones of influence, with little regard for the populations living there.

Three incompatible promises had been made, and the resulting contradictions planted the seeds of a conflict that has never been resolved. This period of European manipulation in the Middle East deserves attention from anyone seeking to understand why the conflict has proven so intractable. Much of the modern political geography of the region was shaped not by the people who lived there but by European powers pursuing their own strategic interests. The carving up of the Ottoman Empire after World War I echoed the Berlin Conference of 1885, where European empires divided Africa among themselves with little regard for the people who actually inhabited the continent. The Middle East received similar treatment, and the consequences have been similarly devastating.

1948: The Birth of a Nation and the Birth of a Crisis

On November 29, 1947, the United Nations General Assembly voted to partition Palestine into separate Jewish and Arab states, with Jerusalem placed under international administration. The Jewish leadership accepted the partition plan. The Arab leadership rejected it. On May 14, 1948, the state of Israel declared its independence. For the Jewish people, this was the fulfillment of a two-thousand-year dream, the return to the land God had promised to Abraham, Isaac, and Jacob. For the Palestinian Arabs who had been living in the same territory, it was the beginning of a catastrophe they call al-Nakba, the Arabic word for disaster.

The armies of five Arab nations, Egypt, Jordan, Syria, Lebanon, and Iraq, immediately invaded the newly declared state. Against enormous odds, Israel survived. But the 1948 war that followed resulted in the displacement of approximately 700,000 Palestinians from their homes, creating a refugee crisis that has never been resolved. Entire villages were emptied. Families fled with whatever they could carry, expecting to return within days or weeks. Most never did.

These refugees, and their descendants, now number more than seven million people. The question of what justice looks like for these refugees remains one of the most intractable issues in any peace negotiation. Palestinians demand the "right of return" to the homes their families abandoned in 1948. Israel argues that accepting this demand would mean the end of Israel as a Jewish state, since adding seven million Arabs to a country of roughly eight million people, including 1.5 million Arab citizens already present, would make Jews a minority in their own nation.

This is not a problem with a simple solution. Both sides have legitimate claims rooted in genuine suffering. The Jewish people had just emerged from the Holocaust, the most systematic attempt at genocide in human history, in which six million Jews were murdered by the Nazi regime. Their need for a secure homeland was not abstract. It was existential. At the same time, the Palestinian families who lost their homes, their land, and their communities suffered real and devastating losses that have shaped their identity and their political aspirations for generations.

For the Christian reader, this double reality requires a posture of compassion that resists the temptation to flatten the conflict into a simple narrative with clear heroes and villains. God's covenant with Israel is real, and the prophetic significance of the Jewish return to the land is profound. But God's concern for justice, for the poor, for the displaced, and for those who suffer under oppression is equally real and equally biblical. Holding both truths simultaneously is one of the great challenges of engaging with this conflict from a Christ-centered perspective.

Arab Israelis: Citizens in Name, Strangers in Practice

Palestinians who remained within Israel's borders after 1948, known as "Arab Israelis," were placed under military rule until 1966 and were unable to directly contact family members living in refugee camps. Most were granted Israeli citizenship in 1952, but they faced a host of discriminatory laws that denied them access to their land, limited their economic opportunities, and restricted their movements. While they could vote, form political parties, and hold public office, extensive government surveillance, and punishment of those who criticized the state, created a pervasive climate of fear among these Palestinian citizens of Israel.

Discrimination and economic disadvantage continue today. Palestinian towns and villages in Israel face housing shortages and economic underdevelopment. Hiring practices that require job applicants to live in certain areas or to have served in the military, something very few Palestinian citizens do, end up pushing Palestinians into precarious low-wage jobs. While direct housing discrimination was banned by the courts, Jewish communities often set up admissions committees that effectively limit the number of Palestinian citizens living in majority Jewish towns. This de facto segregation is also reflected in Israel's school system, where students in Arab state schools receive less funding per capita than those in majority Hebrew state schools.

In addition, Palestinian citizens are subjected to discriminatory policing policies. Professionals face everyday forms of prejudice from some Jewish Israeli colleagues who express surprise at their level of education. Palestinian citizens of Israel have been protesting these conditions since the founding of the state, but within strict limits. In 1964, the Arab nationalist Ard group called for *"a just solution for the Palestinian question . . . in accordance with the wishes of the Palestinian Arab people."* In response, the Israeli government banned the group and arrested its leaders on charges of endangering state security.

The Wars That Shaped the Modern Conflict

In the decades following 1948, Israel fought several major wars with its Arab neighbors, each one reshaping the political and territorial landscape of the region. In 1956, the Suez Crisis erupted when Egyptian President Gamal Abdel Nasser nationalized the Suez Canal, which had been controlled by British and French interests. Israel, in coordination with Britain and France, invaded the Sinai Peninsula. Although the military operation was successful, international pressure from both the United States and the Soviet Union forced a withdrawal. The crisis demonstrated the complexity of Cold War dynamics in the region and established Nasser as a hero of Arab nationalism.

The 1967 Six-Day War was a watershed moment. In June of that year, Israel launched a preemptive military strike against Egypt, Syria, and Jordan after weeks of escalating tensions, including the mobilization of Egyptian troops in the Sinai, the closure of the Straits of Tiran to Israeli shipping, and bellicose rhetoric from Arab leaders. In just six days, Israel captured the Sinai Peninsula and the Gaza Strip from Egypt, the West Bank (including East Jerusalem) from Jordan, and the Golan Heights from Syria. The territorial gains were staggering. Israel's land area more than tripled. For many Israelis, the capture of the Old City of Jerusalem, including the Western Wall, was a moment of profound religious and historical significance. For the Arab world, the defeat was humiliating and transformative. For the Palestinians, it meant that hundreds of thousands more people came under Israeli military occupation.

The 1973 Yom Kippur War, launched by Egypt and Syria on the holiest day of the Jewish calendar, caught Israel almost completely by surprise. Egyptian forces crossed the Suez Canal and overran Israeli positions in the Sinai, while Syrian forces advanced into the Golan Heights. For the first few days, Israel's survival appeared genuinely in doubt. A massive American airlift of military supplies, combined with Israeli counterattacks, eventually turned the tide. Israel pushed

Syrian forces back beyond the pre-war lines and established a bridgehead on the western side of the Suez Canal. The war ended in a military stalemate but a political transformation: it demonstrated that Arab armies could challenge Israel and it set the stage for the peace process that followed.

In 1978, Egyptian President Anwar Sadat and Israeli Prime Minister Menachem Begin signed the Camp David Accords, brokered by U.S. President Jimmy Carter. Egypt became the first Arab nation to formally recognize Israel, and Israel returned the Sinai Peninsula to Egypt. The agreement was a landmark achievement, but it came at a terrible cost. Sadat was assassinated by Egyptian military officers in 1981, in part because of his willingness to make peace with Israel. The accords also deepened divisions within the Arab world, as many Arab nations viewed Egypt's decision as a betrayal.

Intifadas, Oslo, and the Collapse of Hope

In December 1987, the First Intifada ("uprising" in Arabic) erupted in the Palestinian territories. Sparked by a traffic accident in Gaza that killed four Palestinian workers, the uprising quickly spread across the West Bank and Gaza Strip. Palestinians engaged in mass protests, strikes, boycotts of Israeli products, and stone-throwing confrontations with Israeli soldiers. The images of Palestinian youth throwing stones at Israeli tanks became iconic symbols of the conflict. Israel responded with a policy of "force, might, and beatings" that drew international condemnation. The First Intifada continued until 1993 and fundamentally changed the dynamics of the conflict by demonstrating that the Palestinian population under occupation was willing to resist, even at great personal cost.

The First Intifada also gave rise to Hamas, the Islamic Resistance Movement, which was founded in 1987 as an offshoot of the Muslim Brotherhood. Hamas opposed the secular approach of the Palestine Liberation Organization (PLO) to the Israeli-Palestinian conflict and rejected any compromise that involved ceding Palestinian territory. From the beginning, Hamas combined social services (schools, clinics, welfare programs) with militant resistance, including suicide bombings that targeted Israeli civilians.

In 1993, the Oslo Accords were signed between Israel and the PLO, establishing a framework for Palestinian self-governance and mutual recognition. The famous handshake between Israeli Prime Minister Yitzhak Rabin and PLO Chairman Yasser Arafat on the White House lawn, witnessed by U.S. President Bill Clinton, seemed to herald a new era of peace. The Palestinian Authority was established, and a process of phased Israeli withdrawal from parts of the West Bank and Gaza was set in motion. For a brief moment, a two-state solution seemed genuinely achievable.

But the promise of Oslo was never fully realized. Israeli settlement construction in the West Bank continued. Palestinian militant attacks on Israeli civilians continued. Trust eroded on both sides. In November 1995, Prime Minister Rabin was assassinated by a right-wing Israeli extremist who opposed the peace process. His death dealt a devastating blow to the hopes that Oslo had raised.

The Second Intifada, which erupted in September 2000, marked the definitive collapse of the Oslo framework. Triggered by a controversial visit by Israeli opposition leader Ariel Sharon to the Temple Mount (known to Muslims as the Haram al-Sharif), the uprising was far more violent than the first. Suicide bombings targeting Israeli buses, restaurants, and nightclubs killed hundreds of Israeli civilians. Israel responded with military incursions into Palestinian cities, targeted assassinations of militant leaders, and the construction of a massive separation barrier that cut deep into West Bank territory. By the time the violence subsided in 2005, more than

3,000 Palestinians and more than 1,000 Israelis had been killed. The peace process was in ruins, and the political landscape had shifted decisively toward hardliners on both sides.

Gaza: The Humanitarian Catastrophe

In 2005, Israel unilaterally withdrew its military forces and civilian settlers from the Gaza Strip. The following year, Hamas won parliamentary elections in the Palestinian territories, and in 2007, after a brief civil war with the Fatah-dominated Palestinian Authority, Hamas seized full control of Gaza. Israel and Egypt imposed a blockade on the territory that has continued in various forms ever since.

The situation within Gaza illustrates the humanitarian dimension of the conflict with painful clarity. Gaza is one of the most densely populated areas on earth, home to approximately two million people in a territory roughly 25 miles long and six miles wide. Its residents have endured decades of blockade, periodic military operations, and chronic economic deprivation. Unemployment has routinely exceeded 40 percent, and access to clean water, electricity, and medical supplies has been severely restricted.

The December 2008 to January 2009 offensive, known as Operation Cast Lead, claimed approximately 1,300 Palestinian lives, the majority of them civilians, including some 400 children. Another 5,000 people were injured, including some 1,800 children and 800 women. Thirteen Israelis, three of them civilians, were also killed. The offensive left much of Gaza in ruins, with a humanitarian crisis that left tens of thousands homeless and hundreds of thousands without access to clean water.

Subsequent military operations followed a similar pattern. Operation Pillar of Defense in 2012 and Operation Protective Edge in 2014 each resulted in significant Palestinian civilian casualties and massive destruction of civilian infrastructure. The 2014 operation alone killed more than 2,200 Palestinians, including more than 500 children, and left approximately 100,000 people homeless. Seventy-three Israelis, including six civilians, were also killed. Each escalation deepened the humanitarian crisis, hardened political positions on both sides, and further eroded any remaining trust in the possibility of a negotiated peace.

America's Wars and the Geopolitics of Oil

The broader geopolitical context has compounded the difficulty of resolving the conflict. The Cold War drew the United States and the Soviet Union into the region as competing patrons, with America supporting Israel and the Soviets arming Arab states. After the Cold War ended, the Iraqi invasion of Kuwait on August 2, 1990, marked the beginning of what some historians have called America's "endless wars" in the Middle East. Before that point, American combat operations in the region had been generally temporary and short-term. President George H.W. Bush wanted to continue that pattern, but it did not work out that way. Four American presidents have now grappled with the challenge of bringing stability to the region, and none has succeeded.

What makes the Palestinian-Israeli conflict a particularly sensitive issue is the horrendous suffering the Jewish people experienced in Christian Europe during World War II. Any criticism of Israeli policies toward the Palestinian people often lends itself to an automatic label of anti-Semitism, making honest public discourse extraordinarily difficult. In the United States, the Jewish community is well established and has significant influence over many aspects of US foreign policy in the Middle East. Some commentators have suggested that US Zionism is more extreme than that seen in Israel itself.

Prior to the discovery of oil, the main reasons for Western involvement in the Middle East had been religious and agricultural. Christianity, Judaism, and Islam all have roots in the region. During the Cold War, the Soviet threat was used to justify involvement. But in modern times, oil has been the primary economic driver. The discovery of vast oil reserves turned the Middle East into a prize of global economic significance, adding yet another layer of competing interests to an already impossibly complex situation.

The religious dimension makes the conflict unlike any other on earth. Jerusalem is sacred to all three Abrahamic faiths. The Temple Mount, where Solomon built the first temple and where the Dome of the Rock now stands, is among the most contested pieces of real estate in human history. No purely political solution can resolve a dispute that is, at its core, about competing claims to divine favor and sacred ground.

October 7, 2023, and Its Aftermath

On the morning of October 7, 2023, a Jewish holiday (Simchat Torah), Hamas launched the most devastating attack on Israeli soil since the founding of the state. In a coordinated assault, thousands of militants breached the heavily fortified Gaza border fence at multiple points, using a combination of rockets, paragliders, motorcycles, and pickup trucks. They attacked Israeli military bases, overran security checkpoints, and stormed civilian communities, including kibbutzim and a music festival in the Negev desert.

The attack killed approximately 1,200 people, including women, children, and elderly civilians. More than 200 people were taken hostage and brought back to Gaza. The scale and brutality of the violence, which included the targeting of entire families in their homes and the massacre of young people at a peace music festival, shocked the world and fundamentally altered the trajectory of the conflict. Israel's military response was swift and overwhelming. Prime Minister Benjamin Netanyahu declared that Israel was "at war" and launched a massive air and ground campaign in Gaza. The subsequent operations resulted in unprecedented destruction of civilian infrastructure, the displacement of nearly the entire population of Gaza, and an immense humanitarian crisis. Hospitals were overwhelmed. Entire neighborhoods were reduced to rubble. The death toll among Palestinian civilians mounted into the tens of thousands, with a significant proportion being women and children.

The international community was deeply divided. The United States reaffirmed its support for Israel's right to self-defense while calling for the protection of civilian lives. Many nations in the Global South condemned what they described as disproportionate military force. Massive protests erupted in cities around the world. The conflict also escalated regionally, with Hezbollah in Lebanon launching attacks on northern Israel, Houthi rebels in Yemen targeting international shipping in the Red Sea, and Iranian-backed militias in Iraq and Syria striking at American forces. For the first time in decades, the possibility of a wider regional war seemed genuinely real.

For students of Scripture, the events of October 7 and their aftermath carry a weight that goes beyond geopolitics. They are a reminder that the conflict described in Genesis, the enmity between the descendants of Isaac and the descendants of Ishmael, is not an ancient curiosity. It is a living, bleeding reality. The prophecies spoken over Ishmael and his descendants have not expired. The covenant promises made to Abraham, Isaac, and Jacob have not been revoked. And the spiritual battle that underlies the physical conflict continues to this day.

The events of recent years have made the subject matter of this book more urgent than ever. Believers across denominations are searching for a biblically grounded framework to understand what is happening. The nightly news provides images, but it does not provide meaning. Politicians offer analysis, but they do not offer hope. Only Scripture can provide both, and it is to Scripture's final word on this conflict that we now turn.

Bible Prophecy and the Future of the Promised Land

God promised that He would regather the nation of Israel and bring them back to the land of their fathers (Jeremiah 3:18; 16:15; Ezekiel 30:42). He promised to protect them from being uprooted or destroyed ever again. In humanity's final battle, described in Scripture as Jacob's trouble, God will save Israel from destruction at the hands of the nations.

The prophet Zechariah described this final confrontation: God will gather all nations against Jerusalem to battle, and the city will face great distress. But then the Lord Himself will go forth and fight against those nations, as He fought in ancient days (Zechariah 14:2-3). By delivering Israel from destruction, God will be sanctified in the eyes of both Israel and the Gentiles (Ezekiel 39:25-27). Through Christ's earthly kingdom, God will establish a New Covenant with the house of Israel and Judah, and under that covenant, all of God's promised earthly blessings will flow, first to the Jew and then to the Gentiles.

Bible prophecy about the Middle East should bring believers hope and comfort, even as we watch the crisis escalate. The embattled Promised Land sits at the crossroads of three continents: Asia, Europe, and Africa. It has been the world's most contested ground for millennia. Historians have noted that more blood has been shed on this narrow strip of land than on any other place on the face of the earth. At the heart of its conflicts is the struggle of three monotheistic religions that claim holy sites within its borders. But it is also the focal point of the supernatural battle between good and evil, and that reality is the essence of its true significance.

For almost two thousand years, the Jewish people wandered among the nations and suffered severe persecution, exactly as the Lord had prophesied in Deuteronomy 28. During all that time, the land lay desolate and cursed, as described in Deuteronomy 29. But in our lifetime, God has begun to regather His people from the four corners of the earth, reestablish them in their land, and transform the wilderness into fruitfulness, as prophesied in Deuteronomy 30. The modern state of Israel, for all its political controversies and moral complexities, stands as tangible evidence that God keeps His promises.

The headlines we read today are not random. They are the outworking of a story that God has been telling since He called Abraham out of Ur. Understanding that story does not make the suffering easier to witness, but it does place the suffering within a framework of meaning that the secular world cannot provide. There is a plan. There is a purpose. And there is a conclusion that is not destruction but redemption. That is the ancient promise, and it is as alive today as the day God first spoke it to a childless old man standing under a canopy of stars.

Chapter 12

THROUGH THE LENS OF THE CROSS

"But now in Christ Jesus you who once were far away have been brought near by the blood of Christ." (Ephesians 2:13)

We have traveled a long road together through these pages. We began with Abraham's calling and traced the story of his divided house through the births of Ishmael and Isaac, through the rivalry of Esau and Jacob, through the twelve tribes and their scattered history, through the great divide between Jew and Gentile, through the ancient roots of the conflict and its modern manifestations. Now, in this final chapter, we must do what the title of this book has promised all along: we must look at everything we have learned through the lens of the cross.

The cross of Jesus Christ is not one lens among many. It is the lens, the interpretive key that unlocks the meaning of every other element in the biblical story. Without the cross, the Abrahamic covenant is a promise without a fulfillment. Without the cross, the division between Jew and Gentile is a wound without a remedy. Without the cross, the Middle East conflict is a tragedy without hope. But with the cross, everything changes.

The Cross as the Center of History

The Bible presents the death and resurrection of Jesus Christ as the central event of human history, the point toward which everything before it was moving and from which everything after it flows. The sacrificial system established through Moses was a shadow of the cross. The covenant promises given to Abraham pointed to the cross.

The prophets who spoke of a Suffering Servant who would bear the sins of many were describing what would happen at the cross. When Jesus cried out, *"It is finished"* (John 19:30), He was not merely announcing the end of His life. He was declaring the completion of a plan that had been in motion since Genesis 3:15, when God first promised that the seed of the woman would crush the head of the serpent. For our purposes, the significance of the cross for the Middle East conflict lies in three realities.

The Cross Reveals God's Heart for All Nations

Jesus did not die for one people group. He died for the world (John 3:16). He died for Jews and for Arabs, for Israelis and for Palestinians, for the descendants of Isaac and the descendants of Ishmael. The covenant promises made to Abraham were never intended to be an end in themselves. They were the means by which God would bless all the families of the earth (Genesis 12:3). The cross is the fulfillment of that universal blessing.

This means that a Christian cannot look at the Middle East conflict and care only about one side. We cannot celebrate the prophetic significance of Israel's return to the land while remaining indifferent to the suffering of Palestinian families. We cannot advocate for Palestinian rights while ignoring the existential security threats that Israel faces. The cross compels a posture of compassion that extends to every person made in the image of God, regardless of which side of the border they were born on.

"Thus saith the Lord of hosts: In those days it shall come to pass, that ten men shall take hold out of all languages of the nations, even shall take hold of the skirt of him that is a Jew, saying, We will go with you: for we have heard that God is with you." (Zechariah 8:23, KJV)

The Cross Addresses the Root of the Conflict

The root of the Israeli-Arab conflict is not primarily territorial. It is spiritual. Land disputes can be negotiated. Borders can be redrawn. But the hatred that Ishmael bore toward Isaac, the bitterness that Esau carried toward Jacob, the centuries of accumulated grievance and retribution, these are matters of the human heart. Only the cross reaches the heart. Only the Gospel can transform an enemy into a brother. Only the power of God that raised Christ from the dead can take the *"wild man"* described in Genesis 16:12 and make him a new creation in Christ (2 Corinthians 5:17).

Consider Paul himself as evidence of this transformative power. He was born Saul of Tarsus, a Hebrew of Hebrews, from the tribe of Benjamin, a Pharisee who described himself as *"extremely zealous for the traditions of my fathers"* (Galatians 1:14). He was present at the stoning of Stephen and led a violent campaign of persecution against the early church. Yet on the road to Damascus, the risen Christ confronted him, and the man who had been a destroyer of the church became its greatest builder. If the cross could transform Saul into Paul, it can transform any heart.

Living Proof: Messianic Jews and Arab Christians

The same transformation has been witnessed in the Middle East in our own time. There are Jewish believers in Jesus, known as Messianic Jews, who worship alongside Arab Christians in communities scattered across Israel and the Palestinian territories. The modern Messianic

Jewish movement, which began to gain momentum in the 1960s and 1970s, now includes an estimated 15,000 to 20,000 believers in Israel alone, worshiping in more than 150 congregations. These believers face unique challenges. Many Jewish families consider conversion to Christianity a betrayal of Jewish identity. Messianic Jews in Israel have faced social ostracism, bureaucratic obstacles to immigration under the Law of Return, and, in some cases, physical threats.

Arab Christians in the Holy Land have an even longer history, tracing their roots to the earliest days of the church. The first Christians were Jews and Arabs living in the same region where Jesus walked. Today, Arab Christians make up a small but significant minority in Israel, the West Bank, and Gaza. They include Greek Orthodox, Roman Catholic, Maronite, Melkite, and Protestant communities. Their numbers have been declining for decades due to emigration, driven by the pressures of living as a minority within a minority, caught between Israeli policies and Islamic social pressure.

When Messianic Jewish and Arab Christian believers gather together for worship, prayer, and fellowship, they embody a reality that the political world considers impossible: genuine reconciliation between Jews and Arabs, grounded not in political compromise but in shared faith in the risen Christ. These congregations are small, often persecuted by both sides, and largely invisible to the mainstream media. But they represent something extraordinary: living proof that the cross can do what politics cannot. When a Jewish believer and an Arab believer break bread together at the Lord's table, the wall of hostility that Ephesians 2 describes is not merely a theological concept. It is a present reality, visible and tangible, in the shared life of a community that exists only because of the Gospel.

The Cross Gives Us a Posture for the Present

So, what does it look like, practically, to engage with the Middle East conflict through the lens of the cross? It means holding several things together that the world insists must be held apart. It means affirming God's covenant faithfulness to Israel while also affirming God's love for the Arab peoples and His desire for their salvation. It means taking biblical prophecy seriously without using it as an excuse for political tribalism. It means praying for the peace of Jerusalem (Psalm 122:6) while also praying for the people of Gaza, of the West Bank, of Lebanon, and of every nation caught in the crossfire.

It means speaking truth in love (Ephesians 4:15). It means being willing to call evil by its name, wherever it appears, without demonizing entire peoples or reducing complex human beings to caricatures. It means recognizing that the politicians and policymakers of this world do not have the tools to resolve a conflict that is ultimately spiritual. Only the Prince of Peace can bring lasting peace to the Middle East. And it means living with hope. Not the shallow optimism that expects everything to work out on its own, but the deep, Scripture-grounded hope that knows the end of the story. God has promised that a day is coming when He will make all things new (Revelation 21:5). A day when the nations will beat their swords into plowshares (Isaiah 2:4). A day when the wolf will lie down with the lamb (Isaiah 11:6). A day when every knee will bow and every tongue will confess that Jesus Christ is Lord (Philippians 2:10-11).

The Cross and the Three Faiths

Throughout this book, we have noted that Judaism, Christianity, and Islam all claim Abraham as a patriarch. The cross is the point where these three traditions diverge most sharply, and it is also, paradoxically, the point where the deepest answers to the conflict reside. Judaism awaits a Messiah who has not yet come. Christianity proclaims a Messiah who has come, died, risen, and will come again. Islam reveres Jesus as a prophet but denies His deity, His death on the cross, and His resurrection. These are foundational claims about the nature of God, the identity of Christ, and the means of salvation.

Although Christianity developed out of Judaic roots, relationships between Jewish and Christian communities have often been strained, particularly in Christian Europe, where Jewish communities were often subject to discrimination and violence at the hands of professing Christians. Today, memorials in Jerusalem (Yad Vashem), in Europe (Auschwitz-Birkenau Memorial and Museum), and in the United States (Holocaust Memorial Museum and Simon Wiesenthal Center) preserve the memory of that persecution. If the church is to be a credible witness for peace, it must acknowledge its own failures.

Christianity has also had a complicated relationship with Islam. The Crusades were an unsuccessful attempt to reverse the Islamic conquest of the Eastern Mediterranean. Islam views Judaism and Christianity as earlier versions of Islam, with revelations given by Allah but misunderstood over time. Muslims see Islam as the final, complete, and correct revelation. According to Muslim beliefs, Muhammad himself is not divine, but a prophet chosen by God to deliver His message. But repentance for past failures is not retreat from truth. The Gospel does not become less true because it has been poorly represented. The Christian calling is to speak the truth about Jesus with humility, clarity, and love.

The Uniting of Two Peoples

In the glory of the Jews, it seemed the Gentiles were forgotten, and in the glory of the Gentiles it seemed the Jews were forgotten. There has always been a division between Jew and Gentile. The Scriptures verify this through the seed of Abraham: Ishmael, the Gentile, the firstborn by the bondwoman Hagar, and Isaac, the Jew, as promised to the free woman. This allegory of Scripture is one believers cannot brush over.

The Apostles John and Paul pointed toward the uniting of these two people through Jesus Christ, the one sacrifice and atonement for all. The believing Gentile is Abraham's seed because Ishmael was Abraham's seed. The promise was made through Ishmael that there would be twelve princes. Under this promise, the church of God presents the twelve Gentile apostles. Even though Isaac was of the circumcision, Ishmael was first circumcised (Genesis 17:20). When the fullness of the Gentiles comes, they are to be a great nation. This greatness is made up of the twenty-four elders: twelve Jewish apostles and twelve Gentile apostles. The second promise made to Ishmael came from God to his mother Hagar:

"Arise, lift up the lad, and hold him in thine hand; for I will make him a great nation. And God opened her eyes, and she saw a well of water; and she went, and filled the bottle with water, and gave the lad drink. And God was with the lad; and he grew, and dwelt in the wilderness, and became an archer." (Genesis 21:18-20, KJV)

Today, the Gentiles drink of that well. It is reaching its fullness for the grafting of the Jews, and they two are becoming one.

A Final Word

We must understand that we live in a fallen world. Great blessings are followed by affliction; victories are followed by temptation; promises are followed by battles. Satan, because his fate is sealed, will not give up any territory without a fight. I began this book by acknowledging that the Middle East conflict is one of the most complex and emotionally charged subjects in both secular and Christian discourse. Having walked through the full narrative, I hope you can see that the complexity, while real, is not without a framework for understanding. The Bible gives us a story, a promise, and a Person.

The story is Abraham's divided house, a family torn apart by impatience, jealousy, and choices made outside God's will. The rivalry between Ishmael and Isaac, the hatred between Esau and Jacob, the scattering of the tribes, the division of Jew and Gentile: these are chapters in a single story of human failure and divine faithfulness. The promise is God's unshakeable commitment to bless all families of the earth through Abraham's seed, partially fulfilled in the history of Israel and fully fulfilled in Jesus Christ. God has kept every promise He has made. The promises that remain unfulfilled will be kept with the same faithfulness.

And the Person is Jesus, the Son of Abraham, the Son of David, the Son of God, in whom every covenant promise finds its *"yes"* and every human division finds its answer. He is the one who wept over Jerusalem (Luke 19:41), who died for the sins of the world, and who will return as a conquering King to establish a kingdom of justice and peace that will never end.

"And in thy seed shall all the nations of the earth be blessed; because thou hast obeyed my voice." (Genesis 22:18, KJV)

"Now to Abraham and his seed were the promises made. He saith not, And to seeds, as of many; but as of one, And to thy seed, which is Christ." (Galatians 3:16, KJV)

The conflict will not be resolved by human effort alone, but it will be resolved. The God who began this story is the God who will finish it—the Alpha and the Omega, the beginning and the end (Revelation 22:13), faithful to complete what He has started (Philippians 1:6). To every pastor, seminary student, Bible study leader, and everyday believer who has read this book: do not be afraid of this conflict. Look at it squarely, through the lens of the cross, and see what God is doing. He is keeping His promises. He is moving history toward its appointed conclusion. And He is calling His church to be a witness, a voice of truth, a channel of compassion, and an embassy of the kingdom that is coming. The house of Abraham is divided, but the God of Abraham is not. He is faithful, He is sovereign, and He is at work. The Promise still stands over a divided house.

AUTHOR'S NOTE

This book began as a doctoral dissertation completed at Canaan Theological Seminary and Bible College in July 2023, titled "Middle East Conflict: Life, Hope, and Truth." The original work was the product of years of theological study, careful scriptural analysis, and a genuine burden for readers to understand one of the most consequential geopolitical and spiritual conflicts in human history. The transformation from academic dissertation to trade books was undertaken with the editorial team at Parker Publishers, whose commitment to preserving the scholarly foundation of the research while making it accessible to pastors, seminary students, small group leaders, and everyday believers has been invaluable.

Since the dissertation was completed, the events of October 7, 2023, and their aftermath have dramatically reshaped the global conversation about the Middle East conflict. These developments have been incorporated into the text, particularly in Chapter 11, to ensure that this book speaks to the moment we are living in and not merely to the moment in which it was originally researched. I am deeply grateful to my wife, Miranda, whose role in my spiritual journey and whose steadfast support made both the dissertation and this book possible. I am grateful to Dr. Karol Hopson, whose tireless dedication to teaching at Canaan Theological Seminary kept me focused and driven. I am grateful to Pastor Scharrod Wills and Overseer Sheldon Wills of True Vine Church of Jesus, whose pastoral guidance and daily prayer have been a constant source of strength. And I am grateful to every reader who has taken the time to walk through these pages with me.

My prayer is that the Lord will use this work to bring clarity, compassion, and hope to a subject that desperately needs all three. May we all learn to look at the Middle East, and at each other, through the lens of the cross.

— Dr. Daniel S. Carrera.

DISCUSSION QUESTIONS FOR SMALL GROUPS AND

BIBLE STUDIES

These questions are designed to encourage thoughtful engagement with the themes of each chapter. They can be used for individual reflection or group discussion. Scripture references are provided to ground the conversation in God's Word.

Chapter 1: Opening the Ancient Family Album

How does understanding the Middle East conflict as a "family story" rather than a political story change the way you engage with it?

What does Abraham's impatience teach us about the consequences of stepping ahead of God's timing in our own lives?

Read Genesis 16:1-2. What parallels do you see between Sarah's decision and decisions you have made when God's promises seemed delayed?

Chapter 2: When Faith Was Young

What surprised you about the shared roots of Islam, Christianity, and Judaism?

How does understanding these connections affect the way you pray for the people of the Middle East?

Read 1 Timothy 3:16. What does this verse reveal about the uniqueness of the Christian claim about Jesus?

Chapter 3: The Land God Promised

What is the difference between God giving title to the land and Israel possessing the land?

How does the Mosaic Covenant's conditional language (Deuteronomy 28-30) apply to Israel's experience throughout history?

What does the faithfulness of God's land promises teach us about the reliability of His promises to us?

Chapter 4: Abraham: The Father Who Changed Everything

Why is it significant that Abraham "believed in the LORD, and He accounted it to him for righteousness" (Genesis 15:6)?

How does Abraham's faith speak to your own walk with God, particularly in seasons of waiting?

Read Galatians 3:16. How does Paul's interpretation of the Abrahamic promise change the way you understand the Old Testament?

Chapter 5: The Son of the Bondwoman

How does God's compassion for Hagar and Ishmael in the wilderness challenge simplistic readings of the conflict?

What does it mean that God made promises to both Isaac and Ishmael?

Read Genesis 21:17-19. What does God's response to Hagar teach us about His character?

Chapter 6: The Son of Promise

What does the stolen blessing teach us about the consequences of deception, even when it produces the "right" outcome?

How do we reconcile God's sovereignty with human failure in this story?

Read Genesis 27:28-29. How does this blessing connect to the larger story of the Abrahamic covenant?

Chapters 7-8: The Twelve Tribes

Which tribe's story resonated with you most, and why?

What does the history of tribal division teach us about the dangers of disunity in the body of Christ?

Read 1 Kings 12:16-19. What lessons about leadership and humility can we draw from the division of the kingdom?

Chapter 9: The Great Divide

How does Paul's teaching in Ephesians 2:12-14 change the way you think about the relationship between Jews and Gentiles?

What does it mean for the church today that Christ has "destroyed the barrier, the dividing wall of hostility"?

Read Galatians 3:28. How should this verse shape our attitude toward people of different backgrounds and nationalities?

Chapter 10: Roots of Blood

How does understanding the five prophecies regarding Ishmael help you interpret current events?

What is the significance of the distinction between the Bible and the Quran's accounts of Abraham?

Read Psalm 83:1-8. How does this ancient prayer relate to today's headlines?

Chapter 11: Today's Headlines, Ancient Promises

How do you hold together compassion for both Israeli and Palestinian suffering?

What does it look like to pray for the peace of Jerusalem while also praying for the people of Gaza?

Read Deuteronomy 30:3-5. How does this prophecy speak to the modern state of Israel?

Chapter 12: Through the Lens of the Cross

How does the cross change your posture toward the Middle East conflict?

What practical steps can you take to engage with this conflict in a way that reflects the love of Christ?

Read Philippians 2:10-11. How does the promise of Christ's ultimate victory give you hope in the face of seemingly intractable conflict?

BIBLIOGRAPHY

Biblical and Theological Sources

* Beale, G. K. (2012). Handbook on the New Testament Use of the Old Testament. Grand Rapids: Baker Academic.

* Grudem, Wayne (2012). Understanding the Big Picture of the Bible: A Guide to Reading the Bible Well. Wheaton: Crossway.

* Johnson, Elizabeth A. (1990). Consider Jesus: Waves of Renewal in Christology. New York: Crossroad Publishing.

* Meyer, F. B. (1978). Paul: A Servant of Jesus Christ. Fort Washington: Christian Literature Crusade.

* Nee, Watchman (2000). The Release of the Spirit. Richmond: Christian Fellowship Publishers. ISBN 0-935008-83-7.

* Pitre, Isaac (1982). The Divine DNA: Your Identity with Divinity. Charlotte: LifeBridge Books.

* The Holy Bible, King James Version (KJV). Primary translation used throughout this work.

* The Holy Bible, English Standard Version (ESV). Crossway Bibles. Used for supplementary references.

* The Holy Bible, New King James Version (NKJV). Thomas Nelson Publishers. Used for supplementary references.

* The Holy Bible, New International Version (NIV). Biblica. Used for supplementary references.

* The Holy Bible, New American Standard Bible (NASB). The Lockman Foundation. Used for supplementary references.

Middle East Conflict and Abrahamic Studies

* Maalouf, Tony (2003). Arabs in the Shadow of Israel: The Unfolding of God's Prophetic Plan for Ishmael's Line. Grand Rapids: Kregel Academic and Professional.

* Young, Darrell G. (2005). The Roots of the Israeli-Arab Conflict. Focus on Jerusalem Prophecy Ministry.

* Nassar, Maha (2017). Brothers Apart: Palestinian Citizens of Israel and the Arab World. Stanford: Stanford University Press.

* Nassar, Maha (2021). "Protests by Palestinian Citizens in Israel Signal Growing Sense of a Common Struggle." The Conversation, May 2021.

* Shah, Anup (2000). "Palestine and Israel Introduction." Global Issues. Available at: globalissues.org/article/112/palestine-and-israel-introduction.

* Shah, Anup (2009). "The Gaza Crisis." Global Issues. Available at: globalissues.org/article/773/gaza.

* Beauchamp, Zack (2018). "What Is Zionism?" Vox, November 20, 2018.

World Religions and Comparative Studies

* Bowker, John (1997). World Religions: The Great Faiths Explored and Explained. New York: DK Publishing.

* Boyett, Jason (2016). 12 Major World Religions: The Beliefs, Rituals, and Traditions of Humanity's Most Influential Faiths. Berkeley: Zephyros Press.

* Cherry, Kendra (2020). "Sigmund Freud's Theories about Religion." Verywell Mind. Available at: verywellmind.com.

* Huda (2018). "The World's Muslim Population." Learn Religions. Available at: learnreligions.com/worlds-muslim-population-2004480.

Church History and Early Christianity

* Dunner, Pini (2017). "Why the Talmud Is the Most Important Text in Judaism." The Algemeiner, August 11, 2017.

* Ferguson, Everett. "Persecution in the Early Church: Did You Know?" Christian History, Issue 27. Christianity Today.

Genealogical and Tribal History

* Wilson, Rosa Lou (2019). The Twelve Tribes of Israel. New York: Page Publishing.

* "Twelve Tribes of Israel." Wikipedia. Available at: en.wikipedia.org/wiki/Twelve_Tribes_of_Israel. Consulted for cross-reference purposes.

Research Reports and Data

* Pew Research Center (2016). "Six Facts about Religious Hostilities in the Middle East and North Africa." Pew Research Center, July 7, 2016. Based on 2014 data. Available at: pewresearch.org.

* United Nations Relief and Works Agency for Palestine Refugees (UNRWA). Palestinian refugee statistics and definitions. Available at: unrwa.org.

* Amnesty International. Reports on ethnic cleansing and religious persecution in Iraq, 2014. Referenced in Chapter 2.

* U.S. Department of State. Reports on religious freedom and persecution in the Middle East, 2014. Referenced in Chapter 2.

Additional Works Consulted

* Josephus, Flavius. Antiquities of the Jews. Referenced for Hasmonean dynasty history and tribal genealogies.

* 1 Maccabees and 2 Maccabees. Apocryphal books referenced for Hasmonean dynasty history.

* Herzl, Theodor (1896). Der Judenstaat (The Jewish State). Referenced for the origins of modern political Zionism.

* The Quran. Referenced for comparative analysis of Abrahamic narratives in Islam, particularly the accounts of Ibrahim (Abraham) and Ismail (Ishmael).

* Balfour, Arthur James (1917). The Balfour Declaration. Letter to Lord Rothschild, November 2, 1917. Referenced for the origins of the British commitment to a Jewish national home in Palestine.

* Camp David Accords (1978). Framework for Peace in the Middle East and Framework for the Conclusion of a Peace Treaty between Egypt and Israel. Referenced for the first Arab-Israeli peace agreement.

* Oslo Accords (1993). Declaration of Principles on Interim Self-Government Arrangements. Referenced for the Israeli-Palestinian peace process.

Note: All Scripture quotations, unless otherwise indicated, are taken from the King James Version (KJV) of the Holy Bible. Where other translations are used, the translation is noted parenthetically. All biblical references have been verified for accuracy against the cited translation.

APPENDIX A: COMPLETE TRIBAL GENEALOGIES

The twelve tribes of Israel descend from the twelve sons of Jacob (Israel), born to four mothers: his wives Leah and Rachel, and their handmaids Zilpah and Bilhah. The tribe of Joseph was later divided into two half-tribes named after Joseph's sons, Ephraim and Manasseh, bringing the total number of landed tribes to twelve (the tribe of Levi received no territorial allotment but was given cities throughout the land). The following genealogical reference includes each tribe's mother, Jacob's blessing from Genesis 49, Moses' blessing from Deuteronomy 33 (where applicable), territorial allotment, and prophetic significance.

Sons of Leah

Reuben (Jacob's Firstborn)

Jacob's Blessing: *"Reuben, thou art my firstborn, my might, and the beginning of my strength, the excellency of dignity, and the excellency of power: Unstable as water, thou shalt not excel."* (Genesis 49:3-4)

Territory: East of the Jordan River and the Dead Sea, from the Arnon River in the south, including the plain of Madaba (Joshua 13:15-23).

Prophetic Significance: Lost the birthright due to sin with Bilhah (Genesis 35:22). Declined to participate in wars during the period of the judges. Aided David as part of his mighty warriors. Exiled with the northern tribes in 722 BC.

Simeon

Jacob's Blessing: *"Simeon and Levi are brethren; instruments of cruelty are in their habitations. Cursed be their anger, for it was fierce." (Genesis 49:5-7)*

Territory: Southwest Canaan, bordered by Judah; appears to have been an enclave within Judah's territory.

Prophetic Significance: Cursed for the massacre of the Shechemites (Genesis 34). One of the less significant tribes. Invited by Judah to fight together for their allotted territories (Judges 1). Teaches that unrestrained anger leads to devastating consequences (Proverbs 29:11).

Levi

Jacob's Blessing: *"Simeon and Levi are brethren; instruments of cruelty are in their habitations. I will scatter them in Jacob, and disperse them in Israel." (Genesis 49:5-7)*

Territory: No territorial allotment. Received 48 cities throughout Israel, including six Cities of Refuge (Joshua 13:33; 21:1-42).

Prophetic Significance: Designated as the priestly tribe. Descendants of Aaron served as Kohanim (priests). Divided into Gershonites, Kohathites, and Merarites. Zealous for the Law during the golden calf incident (Exodus 32). Moses, Eli, Ezra, and John the Baptist descended from Levi.

Judah

Jacob's Blessing: *"The sceptre shall not depart from Judah, nor a lawgiver from between his feet, until Shiloh come; and unto him shall the gathering of the people be." (Genesis 49:10)*

Territory: Southern Canaan, the largest tribal territory, including Jerusalem, Bethlehem, and Hebron.

Prophetic Significance: The royal tribe. King David and the Davidic dynasty descended from Judah through Perez. Jesus Christ, "the Lion of the tribe of Judah" (Revelation 5:5), descended from Judah's line. The Southern Kingdom bore Judah's name, and the term "Jew" derives from Judah.

Issachar

Jacob's Blessing: *"Issachar is a strong ass couching down between two burdens: And he saw that rest was good, and the land that it was pleasant; and bowed his shoulder to bear, and became a servant unto tribute." (Genesis 49:14-15)*

Territory: South of the Sea of Galilee, in the fertile Jezreel Valley.

Prophetic Significance: Known for men who "understood the times and knew what Israel should do" (1 Chronicles 12:32). Territory conquered by Assyria around 720 BC. Teaches principles of work, wisdom, and discernment.

Zebulun

Jacob's Blessing: *"Zebulun shall dwell at the haven of the sea; and he shall be for an haven of ships; and his border shall be unto Zidon." (Genesis 49:13)*

Territory: Northern Israel, in the region later known as Galilee. Bordered the Mediterranean coast area.

Prophetic Significance: Failed to drive out the Canaanites from Kitron and Nahalol (Judges 1:30). Fought valiantly with Deborah and Barak (Judges 4-5). Isaiah prophesied that Galilee (including Zebulun) would be honored as the first to hear Christ's preaching (Isaiah 9:1-2). Much of Jesus' earthly ministry took place in Zebulun's territory.

Sons of Rachel

Joseph (Ephraim and Manasseh)

Jacob's Blessing: *"Joseph is a fruitful bough, even a fruitful bough by a well; whose branches run over the wall." (Genesis 49:22)*

Territory: Ephraim: Central hill country of Canaan, west of the Jordan. Manasseh: Split territory, half east of the Jordan (Transjordan) and half west in central Canaan (Joshua 16-17).

Prophetic Significance: Joseph received the double portion after Reuben's disqualification. Jacob blessed Ephraim above Manasseh (Genesis 48:5-21). The name "Ephraim" often represents the entire Northern Kingdom in prophetic literature (Hosea 5:3; Ezekiel 37:16). Gideon, one of Israel's greatest judges, was from Manasseh.

Benjamin

Jacob's Blessing: *"Benjamin shall ravin as a wolf: in the morning he shall devour the prey, and at night he shall divide the spoil." (Genesis 49:27)*

Territory: Small territory between Judah and Ephraim, including the city of Jerusalem's northern outskirts (Joshua 18:11-28).

Prophetic Significance: Nearly destroyed in the civil war of Judges 19-21. Produced King Saul, Israel's first king, and the Apostle Paul (Philippians 3:5). Remained loyal to the house of David with Judah after the kingdom divided. In Revelation 7:8, 12,000 from Benjamin will be sealed during the tribulation. Benjamin's gate is named in the New Jerusalem (Revelation 21:12-13).

Sons of Bilhah (Rachel's Handmaid)

Dan

Jacob's Blessing: *"Dan shall judge his people, as one of the tribes of Israel. Dan shall be a serpent by the way, an adder in the path, that biteth the horse heels, so that his rider shall fall backward." (Genesis 49:16-17)*

Territory: Originally allotted territory between Judah and Ephraim on the Mediterranean coast (Joshua 19:40-48). Later migrated north and captured Laish, renaming it Dan (Judges 18).

Prophetic Significance: Samson was from Dan (Judges 13-16). After relocating north, the tribe became associated with idolatry (Judges 18:30-31; 2 Kings 10:29). Notably absent from the list of sealed tribes in Revelation 7, which has generated significant theological discussion.

Naphtali

Jacob's Blessing: *"Naphtali is a doe set free that bears beautiful fawns." (Genesis 49:21)*

Territory: Northern Israel, bordering Asher's territory, with the Sea of Kinnereth (Galilee) at its southern edge (Joshua 19:32-39).

Prophetic Significance: Barak, who led 10,000 against the Canaanites, was a Naphtalite (Judges 4:6). Failed to drive out all Canaanites (Judges 1:33). Isaiah prophesied that Naphtali would be honored: "In the future he will honor Galilee of the Gentiles" (Isaiah 9:1). Jesus' ministry in Galilee fulfilled this prophecy. All Jesus' disciples except Judas came from Galilee.

Sons of Zilpah (Leah's Handmaid)

Gad

Jacob's Blessing: *"Gad, a troop shall overcome him: but he shall overcome at the last."* *(Genesis 49:19)*

Territory: East of the Jordan, north of Reuben's territory, in the region of Gilead (Joshua 13:24-28).

Prophetic Significance: Settled east of the Jordan as livestock grazers. Built an altar as "A Witness Between Us, that the LORD is God" (Joshua 22:34). Faithful to their commitment to help conquer Canaan before settling. Exiled in 722 BC. Teaches fidelity to God and to commitments made to others.

Asher

Jacob's Blessing: *"Out of Asher his bread shall be fat, and he shall yield royal dainties."* *(Genesis 49:20)*

Territory: Along the Mediterranean coast in northwestern Canaan (Joshua 19:24-31).

Prophetic Significance: Failed to drive out the Canaanites (Judges 1:31-32). Did not join Deborah and Barak's battle (Judges 5:17). Later responded to Gideon's call (Judges 6:35) and accepted Hezekiah's Passover invitation (2 Chronicles 30:11). Anna the prophetess, who recognized the infant Jesus in the temple, was from Asher (Luke 2:36).

APPENDIX B: KEY COVENANT PASSAGES

The following passages represent the major covenant texts referenced throughout this book, presented in full from the King James Version and organized chronologically. These passages form the scriptural backbone of the Abrahamic covenant, the Mosaic (Land) covenant, the Davidic covenant, and the New Covenant.

The Abrahamic Covenant

Genesis 12:1-3 (The Call and Initial Promise)

"Now the LORD had said unto Abram, Get thee out of thy country, and from thy kindred, and from thy father's house, unto a land that I will shew thee: And I will make of thee a great nation, and I will bless thee, and make thy name great; and thou shalt be a blessing: And I will bless them that bless thee, and curse him that curseth thee: and in thee shall all families of the earth be blessed."

Genesis 13:14-17 (The Land Promise Expanded)

"And the LORD said unto Abram, after that Lot was separated from him, Lift up now thine eyes, and look from the place where thou art northward, and southward, and eastward, and westward: For all the land which thou seest, to thee will I give it, and to thy seed for ever. And I will make thy seed as the dust of the earth: so that if a man can number the dust of the earth, then shall thy seed also be

numbered. Arise, walk through the land in the length of it and in the breadth of it; for I will give it unto thee."

Genesis 15:4-6, 18 (The Covenant of Stars and Boundaries)

"And, behold, the word of the LORD came unto him, saying, This shall not be thine heir; but he that shall come forth out of thine own bowels shall be thine heir. And he brought him forth abroad, and said, Look now toward heaven, and tell the stars, if thou be able to number them: and he said unto him, So shall thy seed be. And he believed in the LORD; and he counted it to him for righteousness. . . . In the same day the LORD made a covenant with Abram, saying, Unto thy seed have I given this land, from the river of Egypt unto the great river, the river Euphrates."

Genesis 17:1-8, 19-21 (The Covenant of Circumcision; Isaac and Ishmael)

"And when Abram was ninety years old and nine, the LORD appeared to Abram, and said unto him, I am the Almighty God; walk before me, and be thou perfect. And I will make my covenant between me and thee, and will multiply thee exceedingly. . . . And I will establish my covenant between me and thee and thy seed after thee in their generations for an everlasting covenant, to be a God unto thee, and to thy seed after thee. And I will give unto thee, and to thy seed after thee, the land wherein thou art a stranger, all the land of Canaan, for an everlasting possession; and I will be their God. . . . And God said, Sarah thy wife shall bear thee a son indeed; and thou shalt call his name Isaac: and I will establish my covenant with him for an everlasting covenant, and with his seed after him. And as for Ishmael, I have heard thee: Behold, I have blessed him, and will make him fruitful, and will multiply him exceedingly; twelve princes shall he beget, and I will

make him a great nation. But my covenant will I establish with Isaac, which Sarah shall bear unto thee at this set time in the next year."

Genesis 22:16-18 (The Oath After the Binding of Isaac)

"By myself have I sworn, saith the LORD, for because thou hast done this thing, and hast not withheld thy son, thine only son: That in blessing I will bless thee, and in multiplying I will multiply thy seed as the stars of the heaven, and as the sand which is upon the sea shore; and thy seed shall possess the gate of his enemies; And in thy seed shall all the nations of the earth be blessed; because thou hast obeyed my voice."

The Promise Extended to Isaac and Jacob

Genesis 26:3-5 (To Isaac)

"Sojourn in this land, and I will be with thee, and will bless thee; for unto thee, and unto thy seed, I will give all these countries, and I will perform the oath which I sware unto Abraham thy father; And I will make thy seed to multiply as the stars of heaven, and will give unto thy seed all these countries; and in thy seed shall all the nations of the earth be blessed; Because that Abraham obeyed my voice, and kept my charge, my commandments, my statutes, and my laws."

Genesis 28:13-15 (To Jacob at Bethel)

"And, behold, the LORD stood above it, and said, I am the LORD God of Abraham thy father, and the God of Isaac: the land whereon thou liest, to thee will I give it, and to thy seed; And thy seed shall be as the dust of the earth, and thou shalt spread

abroad to the west, and to the east, and to the north, and to the south: and in thee and in thy seed shall all the families of the earth be blessed. And, behold, I am with thee, and will keep thee in all places whither thou goest, and will bring thee again into this land; for I will not leave thee, until I have done that which I have spoken to thee of."

Genesis 35:10-12 (The Name Change and Reaffirmation)

"And God said unto him, Thy name is Jacob: thy name shall not be called any more Jacob, but Israel shall be thy name: and he called his name Israel. And God said unto him, I am God Almighty: be fruitful and multiply; a nation and a company of nations shall be of thee, and kings shall come out of thy loins; And the land which I gave Abraham and Isaac, to thee I will give it, and to thy seed after thee will I give the land."

The Mosaic (Land) Covenant

Deuteronomy 28:1, 13-15 (Blessings and Curses)

"And it shall come to pass, if thou shalt hearken diligently unto the voice of the LORD thy God, to observe and to do all his commandments which I command thee this day, that the LORD thy God will set thee on high above all nations of the earth. . . . And the LORD shall make thee the head, and not the tail; and thou shalt be above only, and thou shalt not be beneath; if that thou hearken unto the commandments of the LORD thy God, which I command thee this day, to observe and to do them: And thou shalt not go aside from any of the words which I command thee this day, to the right hand, or to the left, to go after other gods to

serve them. But it shall come to pass, if thou wilt not hearken unto the voice of the LORD thy God, to observe to do all his commandments and his statutes which I command thee this day; that all these curses shall come upon thee, and overtake thee."

Deuteronomy 30:3-5 (The Promise of Restoration)

"That then the LORD thy God will turn thy captivity, and have compassion upon thee, and will return and gather thee from all the nations, whither the LORD thy God hath scattered thee. If any of thine be driven out unto the outmost parts of heaven, from thence will the LORD thy God gather thee, and from thence will he fetch thee: And the LORD thy God will bring thee into the land which thy fathers possessed, and thou shalt possess it; and he will do thee good, and multiply thee above thy fathers."

The Davidic Covenant

1 Chronicles 17:11-14

"And it shall come to pass, when thy days be expired that thou must go to be with thy fathers, that I will raise up thy seed after thee, which shall be of thy sons; and I will establish his kingdom. He shall build me an house, and I will stablish his throne for ever. I will be his father, and he shall be my son: and I will not take my mercy away from him, as I took it from him that was before thee: But I will settle him in mine house and in my kingdom for ever: and his throne shall be established for evermore."

The New Covenant

Jeremiah 31:31-34

"Behold, the days come, saith the LORD, that I will make a new covenant with the house of Israel, and with the house of Judah: Not according to the covenant that I made with their fathers in the day that I took them by the hand to bring them out of the land of Egypt; which my covenant they brake, although I was an husband unto them, saith the LORD: But this shall be the covenant that I will make with the house of Israel; After those days, saith the LORD, I will put my law in their inward parts, and write it in their hearts; and will be their God, and they shall be my people. And they shall teach no more every man his neighbour, and every man his brother, saying, Know the LORD: for they shall all know me, from the least of them unto the greatest of them, saith the LORD: for I will forgive their iniquity, and I will remember their sin no more."

The Fulfillment in Christ

Galatians 3:16, 26-29

"Now to Abraham and his seed were the promises made. He saith not, And to seeds, as of many; but as of one, And to thy seed, which is Christ. . . . For ye are all the children of God by faith in Christ Jesus. For as many of you as have been baptized into Christ have put on Christ. There is neither Jew nor Greek, there is neither bond nor free, there is neither male nor female: for ye are all one in Christ Jesus. And if ye be Christ's, then are ye Abraham's seed, and heirs according to the promise."

APPENDIX C: TIMELINE OF KEY EVENTS

This timeline covers the major biblical, historical, and geopolitical milestones discussed in this book, from the Abrahamic period through the present day. Dates for the biblical period are approximate and follow standard evangelical chronological estimates.

The Patriarchal Period

c. 2166 BC Birth of Abram (Abraham) in Ur of the Chaldees.

c. 2091 BC God calls Abram to leave Ur; Abrahamic Covenant established (Genesis 12).

c. 2080 BC Birth of Ishmael to Abraham and Hagar (Genesis 16).

c. 2066 BC Birth of Isaac to Abraham and Sarah (Genesis 21).

c. 2066 BC Hagar and Ishmael sent away; God promises Ishmael will become a great nation.

c. 2006 BC Birth of Jacob and Esau to Isaac and Rebekah (Genesis 25).

c. 1929 BC Death of Ishmael at age 137 (Genesis 25:17).

c. 1915 BC Jacob's twelve sons born; the twelve tribes begin.

c. 1898 BC Joseph sold into slavery by his brothers (Genesis 37).

c. 1876 BC Jacob's family moves to Egypt during famine.

Exodus Through the Monarchy

c. 1446 BC The Exodus from Egypt under Moses; Mosaic Covenant given at Sinai.

c. 1406 BC Joshua leads Israel into the Promised Land; tribal territories allotted.

c. 1375-1050 BC Period of the Judges. No central government; tribal confederation.

c. 1049 BC Saul anointed as Israel's first king (from the tribe of Benjamin).

c. 1009 BC David becomes king. Reigns from Hebron, then Jerusalem.

c. 971 BC Solomon becomes king. Builds the First Temple in Jerusalem.

c. 931 BC Kingdom divides: Northern Kingdom (Israel) and Southern Kingdom (Judah).

722 BC Assyria conquers the Northern Kingdom. Ten tribes exiled.

586 BC Babylon conquers the Southern Kingdom. Jerusalem and the Temple destroyed.

539 BC Cyrus of Persia allows Jews to return to Jerusalem. Second Temple built.

167-160 BC Maccabean Revolt. Hasmonean dynasty established.

63 BC Roman conquest of Judea. Israel becomes a client kingdom of Rome.

The New Testament Period

c. 4 BC Birth of Jesus Christ in Bethlehem.

c. 30 AD Crucifixion, death, and resurrection of Jesus Christ.

c. 33-60 AD Apostle Paul's missionary journeys; Gospel spreads to Gentile world.

70 AD Roman destruction of the Second Temple. Jewish diaspora begins in earnest.

132-135 AD Bar Kokhba revolt. Romans rename Judea as "Palaestina."

The Islamic Period and Medieval Era

570 AD Birth of Muhammad in Mecca.

622 AD Muhammad's Hijra (migration) to Medina; Islamic calendar begins.

632 AD Death of Muhammad.

638 AD Muslim conquest of Jerusalem under Caliph Umar.

691 AD Dome of the Rock built on the Temple Mount in Jerusalem.

1054 AD East-West Schism divides Christianity into Roman Catholic and Eastern Orthodox.

1095-1291 AD The Crusades. European Christian campaigns to recapture the Holy Land.

1453 AD Fall of Constantinople to the Ottoman Empire.

The Modern Period

1517-1917 Ottoman Empire controls Palestine and much of the Middle East.

1885 Berlin Conference. European powers carve up Africa; precedent for Middle East.

1896 Theodor Herzl publishes Der Judenstaat (The Jewish State).

1897 First Zionist Congress in Basel, Switzerland.

1915-1916 Hussein-McMahon Correspondence. Britain promises Arab independence.

1916 Sykes-Picot Agreement. Britain and France secretly divide Ottoman territories.

1917 Balfour Declaration. Britain supports Jewish national home in Palestine.

1920-1947 British Mandate over Palestine.

1933-1945 The Holocaust. Six million Jews murdered by the Nazi regime.

Nov 29, 1947 UN votes to partition Palestine into Jewish and Arab states.

May 14, 1948 State of Israel declares independence. Five Arab armies invade.

1948-1949 Arab-Israeli War. 700,000 Palestinians displaced (al-Nakba).

1956 Suez Crisis. Israel, Britain, France invade Egypt's Sinai.

June 1967 Six-Day War. Israel captures Sinai, Gaza, West Bank, Golan Heights, East Jerusalem.

Oct 1973 Yom Kippur War. Egypt and Syria attack Israel; eventual stalemate.

1978 Camp David Accords. Egypt becomes first Arab nation to recognize Israel.

1981 Anwar Sadat assassinated by Egyptian military officers.

1987 First Intifada begins. Hamas founded.

1993 Oslo Accords signed. Rabin-Arafat handshake at the White House.

1995 Israeli PM Yitzhak Rabin assassinated by right-wing Israeli extremist.

Sept 2000 Second Intifada begins after Sharon's visit to the Temple Mount.

2005 Israel withdraws from Gaza. Second Intifada ends.

2007 Hamas seizes control of Gaza after civil war with Fatah.

Dec 2008-Jan 2009 Operation Cast Lead. ~1,300 Palestinians killed in three-week offensive.

2012 Operation Pillar of Defense in Gaza.

2014 Operation Protective Edge. 2,200+ Palestinians killed, including 500+ children.

June 2014 ISIS declares caliphate in parts of Iraq and Syria.

Oct 7, 2023 Hamas attacks Israel. ~1,200 killed. 200+ taken hostage.

Oct 2023-present Israeli military operations in Gaza. Massive civilian casualties and displacement.

Oct 2023-present Regional escalation: Hezbollah (Lebanon), Houthis (Yemen), Iranian-backed militias.

APPENDIX D: GLOSSARY OF TERMS

Abrahamic Covenant: The unconditional covenant God made with Abraham, promising him numerous descendants, a specific land (from the river of Egypt to the Euphrates), and that through his seed all nations would be blessed (Genesis 12, 15, 17).

Aliyah: Hebrew for "ascent." Refers to Jewish immigration to the land of Israel. The concept has both spiritual and political dimensions.

Allah: The Arabic word for God. Used by Muslims to refer to the deity of Islam. Arab Christians also use the word Allah to refer to God.

Anti-Semitism: Hostility, prejudice, or discrimination against Jewish people. Has manifested throughout history in pogroms, legal discrimination, social exclusion, and genocide.

Arab League: A loose confederation of twenty-two Arab nations founded in 1945. Its broad mission is to improve coordination among member states on matters of common interest.

Balfour Declaration: A 1917 statement by British Foreign Secretary Arthur Balfour expressing support for the establishment of a Jewish national home in Palestine.

Caliphate: An Islamic state or institution of public office governed under Islamic law by a caliph, who is considered a political and religious successor to Muhammad.

Camp David Accords: The 1978 peace agreements between Egypt and Israel, brokered by U.S. President Jimmy Carter. Egypt became the first Arab nation to recognize Israel.

Christendom: The collective culture of Christian states and communities. Historically refers to the geographic and political reach of Christianity, particularly during the Middle Ages.

Covenant (Conditional): An agreement binding on both parties. Both parties must fulfill their obligations for the covenant to remain in effect. Also called a bilateral covenant.

Covenant (Unconditional): An agreement in which only one party bears the obligation. God's promise stands regardless of the other party's response. Also called a unilateral covenant.

Davidic Covenant: God's promise to King David that his dynasty would endure forever (1 Chronicles 17:11-14). Fulfilled ultimately in Jesus Christ, "the Son of David."

Diaspora: The dispersion of Jewish people outside of the land of Israel, beginning with the Babylonian exile and continuing through the Roman destruction of the Second Temple in 70 AD.

Edomites: Descendants of Esau (also called Edom), Jacob's twin brother. Settled in the southern part of present-day Jordan. Historical enemies of Israel.

Gentile: A non-Jewish person. From the Hebrew goyim ("nations") and Greek ethne ("peoples"). In biblical usage, refers to anyone outside God's covenant people Israel.

Goyim: Hebrew word meaning "nations" or "peoples." Used to refer to non-Jewish nations and, by extension, to non-Jewish individuals.

Hajj: The annual Islamic pilgrimage to Mecca. One of the five pillars of Islam. Required of all Muslims who are physically and financially able to make the journey.

Hamas: The Islamic Resistance Movement. A Palestinian nationalist and Islamist movement founded in 1987, dedicated to the establishment of an Islamic state in historical Palestine.

Hasmonean Dynasty: Jewish ruling dynasty from approximately 140 BC to 63 BC, established after the Maccabean Revolt against the Seleucid Empire.

Hebrew: A descendant of Abraham. The word may derive from "Eber" (Genesis 10:24) or from a root meaning "from the other side." Abraham is the first person called a Hebrew in the Bible (Genesis 14:13).

Holocaust: The systematic, state-sponsored murder of approximately six million Jews by the Nazi regime during World War II (1933-1945).

Id Al-Adha: "The Sacrifice Festival." An Islamic holiday commemorating Abraham's willingness to sacrifice his son. Muslims celebrate the sacrifice of Ishmael; the Bible records the sacrifice of Isaac.

Intifada: Arabic for "uprising" or "shaking off." Refers to two Palestinian uprisings against Israeli occupation: the First Intifada (1987-1993) and the Second Intifada (2000-2005).

Ishmaelites: Descendants of Ishmael, Abraham's firstborn son through Hagar. Associated with the Arab peoples.

Israelites: The physical descendants of Abraham through Isaac and Jacob. Also called the children of Israel, the twelve tribes, or the Hebrew people.

Jihad: Arabic for "struggle" or "striving." In Islamic theology, can refer to an inner spiritual struggle or an outer military struggle. Often translated as "holy war" in Western usage.

Kohanim: The priestly class in Judaism, descended from Aaron, the brother of Moses. Served in the Temple in Jerusalem.

Levant: The eastern Mediterranean region, including modern Israel, Lebanon, part of Syria, and western Jordan. In antiquity, the southern Levant was called Canaan.

Levirate Marriage: The custom by which a man was obligated to marry the widow of his deceased brother if the brother had no sons (Deuteronomy 25:5-10).

Mahdi: "The rightly guided one." In Islamic eschatology, a messianic figure expected to appear before the Day of Judgment to establish justice on earth.

Messianic Jews: Jewish people who believe that Jesus (Yeshua) is the promised Messiah. Maintain Jewish cultural identity while affirming Christian faith.

Mosaic Covenant: The covenant God made with Israel through Moses at Mount Sinai, including the Ten Commandments and the Law. Also called the Sinai Covenant.

Nakba: Arabic for "catastrophe." Refers to the displacement of approximately 700,000 Palestinians during the 1948 Arab-Israeli War.

New Covenant: The covenant promised in Jeremiah 31:31-34, in which God writes His law on the hearts of His people. Christians understand this covenant as fulfilled through Jesus Christ.

Oslo Accords: The 1993 peace agreements between Israel and the PLO, establishing a framework for Palestinian self-governance and mutual recognition.

Palestine: Historical name for the region between the Mediterranean Sea and the Jordan River. The name was applied by the Romans after 135 AD. In modern usage, refers to the Palestinian territories (West Bank and Gaza).

PLO (Palestine Liberation Organization): A political organization founded in 1964 to represent the Palestinian people. Led by Yasser Arafat from 1969 until his death in 2004.

Quran: The holy book of Islam, believed by Muslims to be the direct and final revelation of God (Allah) as delivered to the Prophet Muhammad.

Shahada: The Islamic profession of faith: "There is no god but Allah, and Muhammad is the messenger of Allah." The first of the five pillars of Islam.

Tawhid: The Islamic concept of the absolute oneness of God. Strict monotheism.

Tanakh: The Jewish Scriptures, comprising three sections: Torah (Law), Nevi'im (Prophets), and Ketuvim (Writings). Corresponds to the Christian Old Testament.

Temple Mount: The platform in Jerusalem's Old City where Solomon built the First Temple and Herod rebuilt the Second Temple. Sacred to Judaism, Christianity, and Islam. The Dome of the Rock and Al-Aqsa Mosque now stand on the site.

Torah: The first five books of the Bible (Genesis, Exodus, Leviticus, Numbers, Deuteronomy). Also called the Pentateuch or the Law of Moses.

Zionism: The political movement advocating for the establishment and maintenance of a Jewish state in the biblical Promised Land. Named after Zion, a hill in Jerusalem.

THE END.